WOMEN
IN THE
CRIMINAL
JUSTICE
SYSTEM

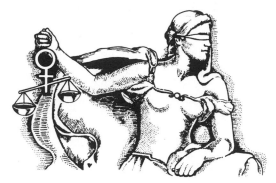

WOMEN
IN THE
CRIMINAL
JUSTICE
SYSTEM

CLARICE FEINMAN

PRAEGER

PRAEGER SPECIAL STUDIES • PRAEGER SCIENTIFIC

Library of Congress Cataloging in Publication Data

Feinman, Clarice.
   Women in the criminal justice system.

   Includes bibliographical references and index.
      1.   Women--Correctional personnel--United
States.   2.   Women prisoners--United States.
3.   Female offenders--United States.   4.   Women
lawyers--United States.   5.   Sex discrimination
against women--United States.   6.   Sex role.
I.   Title.
HV6791.F44   364'.088042   80-12539
ISBN 0-03-052561-6

ISBN 0-03-052566-7 (pbk.)

Published in 1980 by Praeger Publishers
CBS Educational and Professional Publishing
A Division of CBS, Inc.
521 Fifth Avenue, New York, New York 10017 U.S.A.

© 1980 by Clarice Feinman

0123456789   145   98765432

Printed in the United States of America

PREFACE

Women in the criminal justice system (criminals, correction officers, police officers, lawyers, and judges), are poorly understood by the public. Casual and sometimes sensational exposure in the news media does not provide the kind of information that makes for understanding. Even when discussed by the academy or by the government, explanations of the behavior of women are often distorted by a reliance on traditional beliefs about the nature of women and their place in society. As a result there exists much misinformation, simplification, and a great tendency to rely on stereotypes and superficial theories to interpret the words and actions of women.

Unfortunately, there is still relatively little material available examining women in the criminal justice system. Information in newspapers and magazines is based on little real evidence and usually either repeats old stereotypes or uncritically accepts new ones. Most of the scholarly literature since the 1960s focuses on women criminals and women in prisons. The professionals in the system have received less attention: a few books on policewomen and lawyers and none dealing with women as correction officers. Articles in journals cover some areas but ignore others.

This book has been written to provide a more reliable source of information on women in the criminal justice system. At the most obvious level, it gathers material from many different sources and offers a wide-ranging examination of the current situation and the historical factors that produced it. At another level, it interprets this information according to ideas more in harmony with the facts and less influenced by traditional stereotypes. It is an attempt to see women in criminal justice from a fresh perspective, outside the narrowly defined ideas that have predominated until very recently.

To some degree, this book owes a debt to the civil rights movement of the 1960s, which challenged stereotypes about black Americans and thus called into questions stereotypes about other groups. It also owes much to the women's movement, which has questioned the accepted role of women. It owes most, however, to actual experiences and observations centered on the New York City Correctional Institution for Women on Rikers Island, and to conversations with prisoners, correctional personnel in jails, prisons, and departments of correction, and to police personnel, lawyers, and judges in a number of cities. For, in the final analysis, theories and statistics are valuable only if they correspond with the realities of life in prisons, police stations, and courtrooms.

ACKNOWLEDGMENTS

Many people took time to answer my questions and share their experiences as prisoners, professionals, and researchers in the criminal justice system. I want to thank them: Cynthia Anderson, Sybil Brand Institute, Los Angeles; Mike Aun, Federal Bureau of Prisons; Arlene Becker, California Department of Corrections; Jessie Behagen, former superintendent, New York City House of Detention for Women; Osa Coffey, American Correctional Association; Debora Cohn, New York City Department of Correction; Linda Feinberg, Department of Criminal Justice, Trenton State College; Florence Holland, former superintendent, New York City House of Detention for Women; Zona Hostetler, Washington, D.C. Bar Association; Anna M. Kross, former lawyer, magistrate judge and commissioner of correction, New York City; Donna Lenfall, Women's Legal Defense Fund; Linda Lengyel, Department of Criminal Justice, Trenton State College; Mary Lindsay, former superintendent, New York City House of Detention for Women; Richard Lyle, Federal Bureau of Prisons; Sherry MacPhearson, Correctional Institution for Women, Clinton, New Jersey; William McClammy, New Jersey Department of Corrections Training Academy; Ann McCrory, Judicial Selection Project; Theresa Melchionne, former detective and deputy commissioner in charge of community relations, New York City Police Department; Marie Miller, New Jersey Department of Corrections Training Academy; Betty Minor, Center for Women's Policy Studies; Essie Murph, former superintendent, New York City Correctional Institution for Women; Ann Powers, president, New York City Policewomen's Endowment Association; Laural Rans, National Association of Women in Criminal Justice; Karen Reilly, CONtact Center; Sam Samples, Federal Bureau of Prisons; David Schaitberger, Bureau of Census; Felicia Shpritzer, former lieutenant, New York City Police Department; Barbara Studerman, American Association of Law Schools; Cynthia Sultan, Police Foundation; Jean Wolfe, California Department of Corrections; Women Inmates, New York City Correctional Institution for Women; Anna Zaremba, Connecticut Department of Corrections Training Academy.

I am deeply grateful to those who read the manuscript and offered invaluable suggestions: William Zeisel, editor, *Trends in History*, the publication of the Institute for Research in History; Lynda Sharp, editor, Praeger Publishers; Claudine Schweber, Department of Criminal

Justice, Buffalo State University College; David Reimers, Department of History, New York University.

To my children, Shirley and Jonathan, who offered words of encouragement, thank you.

No words can express the depth of my feeling for my friend Bert, who was always there when I needed him.

CONTENTS

WOMEN
IN THE
CRIMINAL
JUSTICE
SYSTEM

— *One*—

INTRODUCTION

In the modern criminal justice system women are viewed according to attitudes that derive in large measure from classical Greece and Rome and medieval Europe. Both pagan mythology and Judeo-Christian theology present women with a dual nature, either as madonnas, or as whores.

THE MADONNA/WHORE DUALITY

The dual perception seems to have arisen from the two sharply different ways in which female sexuality affected men. On the one hand, women produced children, which was good and necessary for the survival of the family and community. Exactly how this was done was a mystery, although it was known somehow to relate to the equally mysterious phenomenon of menstruation. On the other hand, women inflamed men's passions and prompted them to lose control of themselves, again in ways that were often difficult to explain. Clearly women were different from men and possessed unique powers that made them both necessary and dangerous. It was not surprising that men, in their effort to come to terms with female sexuality, should categorize women according to the degree to which they fit one role or the other, either madonna or whore.[1]

In the Old and New Testaments, a good woman helps her man and is submissive and loyal; Ruth said, "Whither thou goest, I will go."[2] A good

1

woman, as in the Song of Solomon, brings life: "Thy belly is like a heap of wheat, set about with lilies."[3] The evil nature of women destroys men by using sex, just as Delilah robbed Samson of his strength and betrayed him. Ecclesiasticus warned, "Wine and women will make men of understanding to fall away."[4]

This concern over the potentially destructive nature of women provided the basis for persistent beliefs that women were morally, physically, and intellectually inferior to men. Zeus showed his superiority over women by giving birth to Athena and Dionysus, usurping from female divinities their unique procreative powers. Pandora, the first woman, according to Greek mythology, could not resist the urge to open the mysterious box given her as a marriage gift; out of it flew all the evils of this world, leaving behind only Hope. Similarly, in the Old Testament it was a woman who ate the forbidden fruit and caused the fall from Paradise.[5]

Implicit in the madonna/whore duality is women's subservience to men, who assumed the role of protectors of the madonnas and punishers of the whores. Eve was created from Adam's rib because it was "not good that the man should be alone; I will make a helpmeet for him."[6] In the New Testament Paul declared that "the man is not of the woman; but the woman is of the man. Neither was the man created for the woman; but the woman for the man."[7]

WOMEN'S CRIMES AND PUNISHMENTS

The inferiority of women and their division along the madonna/whore duality were major factors in defining the nature of female criminal behavior. In classical Greece and Rome and medieval Europe, the primary role of the proper woman was as the mother of legitimate male heirs for the continuance of her husband's name and property. A virgin maid was valued because through a marriage contract she became the medium of exchange for wealth and power. Adultery was therefore a serious crime for a woman of a propertied marriage, since it threatened the purity and the legitimacy of the next generation. An adulterous wife could be put to death, and a husband who killed his wife and her lover in flagrante delicto suffered no legal penalty. ("Paramour homicide" remains a legitimate legal defense even today.)[8]

Different standards prevailed among the lower-class women and slaves, many of whom were prostitutes or "loose" women. Prostitution was condoned by Greco-Roman society and tolerated by the medieval church, as long as the women were of lower-class origin. Even in modern times brothels operated quite openly in many countries. In England during the eighteenth century, proponents of public brothels argued that such establishments would protect women and children from venereal disease if the prostitutes were examined by government medical officials. Only with the great reform movements of the Victorian era did the brothels go underground and prostitution become a crime.[9]

Unlike adultery and prostitution, which tended to follow class divisions, infanticide touched all women. In the Greco-Roman world the exposure of unwanted infants, usually in places specifically set aside for the purpose, was a legal and socially acceptable means of regulating family size and composition. The spread of Christianity, which condemned infanticide as a form of murder, gradually did away with exposure, but new forms of infanticide arose. Studies of infanticide in England in the thirteenth and fourteenth centuries attest to the common occurrence of "overlaying," suffocation of the child being nursed when the mother rolled the wrong way. If the mother was married and living with her husband she was rarely punished, except perhaps with a public remonstrance. But the unmarried mother might be labeled a witch and could be stoned to death or buried alive.[10]

Yet another group of female offenses emerged in the sixteenth century, as the growth of commerce and urbanism produced large numbers of homeless people who had no regular livelihood. Paupers moving from parish to parish and town to town created a social and financial burden and contributed to the incidence of prostitution, theft, and more serious crimes. A common response was to make poverty a crime punishable by incarceration. In England, to cite one case, a series of poor laws were enacted. Vagrants and paupers with no home or employment were whipped, branded, driven from the towns, enslaved for up to two years, or placed in workhouses where they worked at spinning and carding wool or mending. Unmarried mothers were sent to houses of correction as a punishment because their illegitimate children were charges on the parish. If they continued to have bastards they were returned to houses of correction until they were deemed reformed. By the Act of 1661, the government authorized contractors to transport women from the workhouses and houses of correction to the American colonies. Some of the women were thieves and prostitutes, but others, perhaps a goodly number, were guilty only of poverty, indebtedness, or unemployment. In contrast, upper-class women offenders could take advantage of "Benefit of Clergy," which allowed them to do penance or serve the church in lieu of confinement in a prison or workhouse; they thus were able to remain free and live with their families.[11]

WOMEN REFORMERS

In addition to punishment, women offenders also were subject to attempts at reform. The reformers, usually upper-class women, concentrated on the most fallen of women, the prostitutes. Basing their program on Christian teaching and exhortation, they offered as role models their own exemplary lives. In order to accomplish their goals, women reformers tried to isolate the sinners from corrupt elements, primarily men. Residences were established where women offenders could live and learn and where unsullied women could do the reforming and teaching.

One of the earliest attempts to apply these methods of reform took place in the sixth century in the Byzantine empire. The empress Theodora initiated a plan by which over 500 prostitutes were confined in a convent called Repentance (Metanoia) for the purpose of restoring them eventually to the church and the home. Although the project failed, it did establish a precedent. Similar experiments took place in medieval Europe, and by the fourteenth century, with the encouragement of the Church, a Magdalen Home opened in Vienna, where fallen but repentant women could live until they were ready to return to society as good Christians. Magdalen Homes, forerunners of present-day halfway houses, opened in other European cities, and in 1830 the Magdalen Society started a residence, the Magdalen Home, in New York City.[12]

The women who helped reform the prostitutes and other women offenders acted in accord with traditional female roles. They served God and protected the family and community by reforming criminal women. Therefore, although they went beyond the singular homemaker role, they found acceptance in their home, church, and community because they provided a necessary function in dealing with problems in the community. In addition, they were women beyond reproach in terms of their social class and their adherence to traditional values of womanhood.

Women reformers in the United States followed the pattern established in Europe. They were at first mostly from the upper class, white and traditional. They focused on dealing with women and children, attempting to isolate them in homes for the purpose of moral restoration. They did not seek to change the social order but rather to preserve it, and in so doing they gained the respect of the community. Because U. S. culture was Anglo-American, the standards set by reformers were based on values important to white Protestants, and because the reformers came from the upper class, the goals were based on the values of that class.

LAWS DEFINING WOMEN'S PLACE

Both the woman reformer and the woman offender continued to be evaluated and defined in terms of traditional attitudes, and these attitudes were reflected in law. The men who wrote and interpreted the law considered it their responsibility to secure the safety of women, the family, and the community: "That God designed the sexes to occupy different spheres of action, and that it belonged to men to make, apply, and execute the laws was regarded as an almost axiomatic truth."[13] It followed that certain areas of life could be entered by women only under carefully controlled circumstances. This was true for employment, where the principle of classification by sex was reinforced in *Muller* v. *Oregon* in 1908. The U.S. Supreme Court declared constitutional the right of states to pass labor laws for the protection of women in specific job categories. The Court based its decision on the traditional belief that woman's biology, her sexual cycle, made her dependent on man. According to Justice Brewer, "That woman's physical structure and the performance of maternal functions place her at a disadvantage in the struggle for subsistence is obvious."[14]

Recognizing that some women had to work, legislators and judges sought to protect womanhood and motherhood, but in reality they harmed women by restricting their ability to work and earn a living on an equal basis with men. Such protection made it difficult for women to have careers in criminal justice, for it reinforced traditional attitudes and thus prevented women from receiving the same work experience, promotions, and financial rewards as men.

That women had to be protected from the sordid facts of life to preserve their purity led to their exclusion from jury duty; even today automatic exemptions are available in many jurisdictions. Exclusion stems from the English common-law precedent that gave the right only to men. In 1869 the U.S. Supreme Court supported the common-law exclusion by deciding that states could constitutionally limit jury duty to men only. Women first gained the right to sit on juries in Utah in 1898. As of June 1975, five states provided an automatic exemption for men or women who could demonstrate that they had legal custody or care of a child, and four states provided automatic exemptions for women. This is despite the U. S. Supreme Court decision in January 1975 in *Taylor* v. *Louisiana* that women could not be excluded from jury duty solely because of sex.[15]

Although women gained the right to serve on federal juries by the

Civil Rights Act of 1957, states have continued to impose restrictions. In *Hoyt* v. *Florida* in 1961, U. S. Supreme Court Justice Harlan, delivering the opinion of the Court, wrote: "Despite the enlightened emancipation of women from the restrictions and protections of bygone years, and their entry into many parts of community life formerly considered to be reserved for men, woman is still regarded as the center of home and family life."[16] Rejecting the federal court decision in *White* v. *Crook* that held exclusion from jury duty a violation of a woman's Fourteenth Amendment right to equal protection, the Mississippi Supreme Court in 1966 upheld the state law "absolutely" excluding women from jury duty. In the court's opinion, "The legislature has the right to exclude women so they may continue as mothers, wives, and homemakers, and also to protect them (in some areas they are still upon a pedestal) from the filth, obscenity and noxious atmosphere that so often pervades a courtroom during a jury trial."[17]

Just as the proper woman, the madonna, had to be protected from the world, so the offender, the whore, had to be punished. But the punishment had to be fitted to the unique nature of women. Thus, traditional attitudes about the nature of women influenced state laws aimed at the sentencing and rehabilitation of women offenders. According to these laws, it was mandatory that women "must" be sentenced for an indeterminate term, whereas men "might" be sentenced for either an indeterminate or a determinate term upon conviction for the same type of crime.

One of the best known examples of such discriminatory legislation was the Muncy Act of Pennsylvania, which stated that any female pleading guilty to or convicted of a crime punishable by imprisonment of one year or more must be sentenced to the state prison for women, and that her sentence "shall be merely a general one... and shall not fix or limit the duration thereof."[18] This meant that compared to men convicted of similar crimes, women often served longer sentences and had to wait longer before becoming eligible for parole.

The rationale for the different treatment of men and women was based on the old view of different natures. This is evident from the opinion of a lower Pennsylvania court, which said in upholding the Muncy Act:

> ... the legislature reasonably could have concluded that indeterminate sentences should be imposed on women as a class, allowing the time of incarceration to be matched to the necessary treatment in order to provide more effective rehabilitation. Such a conclusion could be based on the physiological and psychological makeup of women, the type of crime commited by women, their relationship to the criminal world,

their roles in society, their unique vocational skills and pursuits, and their reaction as a class to imprisonment.[19]

As long as the courts retained these traditional views of women, such laws as the Muncy Act remained in force; but in the 1960s important changes occurred. In 1966 Jane Daniel was convicted in Pennsylvania of robbery, an offense that carried a maximum sentence of ten years. At first the judge sentenced her to one-to-four years in the county prison, but within a month brought her back to court for resentencing under the Muncy Act, which required an indeterminate-to-ten-year term at the Muncy state prison for women. Daniel appealed to the Pennsylvania Supreme Court and won in a precedent-setting case: the law was declared unconstitutional.[20]

Subsequently, similar laws were declared unconstitutional in New Jersey and Connecticut. The New Jersey Supreme Court decided in favor of Mary A. Costello, who argued that her constitutional right of equal protection under the Fourteenth Amendment had been violated when she was sentenced upon pleading guilty to a gambling offense. Based on New Jersey law, a man convicted of the same offense would have received a sentence of not less than one year and not more than two years. Women convicted of that gambling offense received an indeterminate sentence not to exceed five years. In 1973 the court voted in Costello's favor, opening the way to parole for 130 women incarcerated with indeterminate sentences in the state prison for women at Clinton.[21]

THEORETICAL REINFORCEMENT

The unquestioned existence for so many years of laws such as the Muncy Act was greatly abetted by the theoretical writings of several well-known researchers into human behavior. Three in particular have been important during the past 80 years: Cesare Lombroso, Sigmund Freud, and Otto Pollak.

Lombroso, who studied both male and female prisoners in Italy, emphasized the madonna/whore duality and the inferiority of women. That woman is either good or bad is obvious in his statement, "Her normal sister is kept in the paths of virtue by many causes, such as maternity, piety, weakness, and when these counter influences fail, and a woman commits a crime, we may conclude that her wickedness must have been enormous before it could triumph over so many obstacles."[22] He concluded that because women are intellectually, morally, and physically inferior to men, they are less capable than men of engaging in criminal activities other than prostitution. However, if they do they must be "monsters"; abnormal among normal women and abnormal among criminal women.[23]

Freud interpreted women's behavior based on personality. He asserted that women suffered from feelings of inferiority because they lacked a penis. Because of this penis envy, woman had two choices: either marriage and motherhood to give them satisfaction, or aggression and neurosis.[24]

Pollak evaluated women's behavior in terms of the social roles they were expected to play. He argued that men and women have been taught that women must follow specific roles; any other path would be a betrayal of "their womanhood." We are so steeped in the traditional opinion of womanhood, he thought, that we deceive ourselves into thinking that women would not "venture out into a reserve of men" and become criminal.[25] He inferred that women who deny their womanhood become like men, or masculine.

Each writer approached the question of female criminal behavior from his own perspective. However, women's actions were never explained on the same basis as men's. Criminal actions and tendencies among men were typically explained with reference to factors such as poverty, racism, and lack of economic opportunity. Similar actions and tendencies among women were explained by resorting to the concept of the proper or natural female role. Rejection of this role, the writers argued, inevitably leads to deviance, whether as neurosis or as criminal activity. For Lombroso, Freud, and Pollak, the natural inferiority of women only reinforced the harmful effects of the failure to fulfill the proper female role. Modern theoretical writings have in this way given new strength and legitimacy to attitudes dating from ancient and medieval Europe.

The cumulative impact of theory and practice has been profound. Women, whether criminal or professional, have been taught that their one acceptable function is that of wife and mother and their one acceptable place is the home. Most women, fearing rejection from society, have accepted this role, or at least have admitted that is a role to which they ought to aspire. Certainly this was true for U. S. women reformers in the nineteenth century, from whose ranks the first professionals in the criminal justice system came. They were upper-class and conformed at least outwardly to the traditional beliefs.

WOMEN'S MOVEMENT

In the past 20 years, however, changes have occurred in how women perceive themselves, and they have become sufficiently self-conscious and organized to lobby successfully for governmental action against discrimination. One result has been the overturning of laws such as the Muncy Act; another has been to open a great debate on the proper public and private roles of all women, both in and out of the criminal justice system. This debate is the backdrop for many recent developments in corrections, law enforcement, and the legal profession, and accordingly must be taken account of in any consideration of these topics.

The women's movement generally is perceived as attempting to establish the legal right of all persons, regardless of sex, to have an equal opportunity in all aspects of life: work, family, and community. This principle runs counter to many of the roles traditionally ascribed to women, and in this sense the women's movement may be seen as threatening. It is commonly said that if women do not remain in their traditional mother/housewife role, children will become delinquents and husbands not only will be neglected but also diminished in manhood. Theologians, social scientists, and writers in the popular press have all stressed women's responsibility to family and community. In the nineteenth century this was embodied in the "cult of true womanhood," a view that remains enshrined even today. Then and now women have been told that they mold the next generation and therefore should leave affairs outside the home to men.[26]

It is evident that any movement that tries to change these deeply felt values will be met with resistance and hostility, as has been true of the women's movement. Sometimes the opposition is overt, sometimes it is covert, and in many cases it probably is unconscious. It is the nature of fundamental values that they govern thought and action without always being clearly and consciously articulated by the affected individuals. The linkage of the women's movement to crime may well be an example of such unconscious action. That is to say, even objective researchers who might have no public position on the challenge to traditional female roles might still attempt to defend those roles in the face of a challenge. Whatever the motivation of these researchers, it seems very likely that the linkage of the women's movement and criminality is both a defense of traditional roles and an attack on the new ideas.

The women's movement has not been the only threat to traditional roles during the past half century, and it is instructive to compare previous events with the present. Once the question was the introduction of women into the labor force. Women have always worked, but until the 1940s they were drawn primarily from the lower class, which included many immigrants and blacks. They held low status, low paying jobs as domestics, salespersons, and factory and clerical workers. Upper-class white women, the "ladies" of an urban, industrial society, were full-time wives and mothers. Men displayed their prowess in the industrial jungle by being able to afford to have wives who did not have to work.[27]

As long as upper-class and middle-class women did not work, no violence was done to the madonna/whore duality, because lower-class women had never been seen as part of the madonna role. The well-being and delinquency of children from lower-class, working women were serious matters of concern, but it seemed in the national interest to have available the cheap labor of these women and, eventually, of their children.

War brought change. With the labor shortages of the two world wars, all adults, regardless of color, sex, or other distinguishing characteristics, became potential contributors to the common fight. Suddenly it was patriotic for women to leave the home and work in the factory, the office, or in public drives to raise money, scrap, or bandages. In World War I the entry of women into the workforce was rather limited, but in World War II it increased dramatically as over 6 million women worked in all kinds of jobs, even in shipyards, railroads, lumbercamps, and the armed forces.[28]

The end of war brought an equally sudden demand that the new workers put down their tools and make way for the returning men. Almost overnight it became patriotic to become mothers and housewives again. As the head of the National Association of Manufacturers said: "From a humanitarian point of view, too many women should not stay in the labor force. The home is the basic American institution."[29] Sociologists took up the familiar position of before the war: "Women must bear and rear children; husbands must support them."[30]

To a considerable degree women heeded this advice and left the labor force. Nevertheless, precedents had been set, and gradually, beginning in the 1950s, many women with families began to work outside the home. Now, however, the women were not only lower class, but middle class as well. The "ladies" started to combine careers with home life, and unlike the lower-class women they began to ask for their rights, for equality. They were educated and articulate, and constituted a small, identifiable group that gradually achieved some self-awareness. These women were the core of the emerging women's movement and their ideas provided a sense of direction and a measure of what had to be done.[31]

As the movement grew, affecting ever-larger numbers of educated women, the threat to traditional values increased. Men were confronted by a movement that seemed to be increasing the competition for jobs and money. They were disturbed by an apparently liberated female identity that reversed the old roles, and by the specter of a topsy-turvy family in which men did the dishes and women brought home the bacon. Many women who were wives and mothers also felt that their own roles were being threatened and that their husbands' image and livelihood were in jeopardy. The whole process was made even more unsettling because the women who joined the movement were too well educated to be dismissed out of hand and too articulate and committed to be squelched. Since the movement could not be evaded, it had to be confronted, and no one who lived through the 1960s will forget the passion of that debate.

The resolution of the debate has not yet come, but some things are clear. First, the women's movement of today is much more threatening to men than what came before, even the large-scale introduction of women into the workforce during the world wars, because for the first time it has been espoused by large numbers of women who are the intellectual and educational equals of men. Second, because it is more threatening, the movement has engendered stronger and more sophisticated responses. With regard to the criminal justice system, the responses have taken shape at all levels, theoretical and practical, involving the women as offenders, prisoners, corrections officers, police officers, lawyers, and judges. Any examination of these aspects of the criminal justice system therefore must have the women's movement and its attack on the madonna/whore duality as a continuing theme.

NOTES

1. Sarah B. Pomeroy, *Goddesses, Whores, Wives, and Slaves: Women in Classical Antiquity* (New York: Schocken, 1975), pp. 8–9; and Page Smith, *Daughters of the Promised Land: Women in American History* (Boston: Little, Brown, 1970), pp. 1–7.

2. Ruth 1:16.

3. Song of Sol. 7:2.

4. Judg. 16:6, Ecclesiasticus 19:2.

5. Pomeroy, op cit., pp. 2–3.

6. Gen. 2:18.

7. I Cor. 11:8–9.

8. Pomeroy, op. cit., pp. 20–23, 33–35, 62–65, 81–82, 86–88, and 154–160; Vern L. Bullough, *The Subordinate Sex: A History of Attitudes Towards Women* (Baltimore, Md.: Penguin, 1974), pp. 19–120, and 153–194; and Julia O'Faolain and Lauro Martines, eds., *Not in God's Image: Women in History from the Greeks to the Victorians* (New York: Harper Torchbook, 1973), pp. 175–178.

9. Pomeroy, op. cit., pp. 68–70, 86–87, and 164–69; David J. Pivar, *Purity Crusade: Sexual Morality and Social Control, 1868–1900* (Westport, Conn.: Greenwood Press, 1973), pp. 13–17; and J. Johnson, *The Laws Respecting Women* [1777; reprint ed., Dobbs Ferry, N.Y.: Oceana Publications, 1974], p. 300.

10. Marvin Harris, *Cannibals and Kings: The Origins of Culture* (New York: Random House, 1977), pp. 171 and 183–84.

11. Johnson, op. cit., pp. 300 and 302; Walter H. Blumental, *Brides from Bridwell: Female Felons Sent to Colonial America* (Rutland, Vt.: Charles E. Tuttle, 1962), pp. 11–26; and Norman Longmate, *The Workhouse* (New York: St. Martin's Press, 1974), pp. 14–18.

12. Bullough, op. cit., pp. 161–63, and 206–7; O'Faolain and Martines, op. cit., pp. 82–83; and Pivar, op. cit., p. 15.

13. Leon Kanowitz, *Sex Roles in Law and Society: Cases and Materials* (Albuquerque, N.M.: University of New Mexico Press, 1973), p. 44.

14. Ibid., p. 47.

15. Leo Kanowitz, *Women and the Law: The Unfinished Revolution* (Albuquerque, N.M.: University of New Mexico Press, 1969), p. 28; Anne R. Mahoney, "Sexism in Voir Dire: The Use of Sex Stereotypes in Jury Selection," in *Women in the Courts*, ed. Winifred L. Hepperle and Laura Crites (Williamsburg, Va.: National Center for State Courts, 1978), pp. 115–17.

16. Kanowitz, *Sex Roles in Law and Society*, op. cit., p. 76.

17. Ibid., p. 59.

18. Kanowitz, *Women and the Law*, op. cit., p. 167.

19. Ibid., p. 168.

20. Meda Chesney-Lind, "Chivalry Reexamined: Women and the Criminal Justice System," in *Women, Crime, and the Criminal Justice System*, Lee H. Bowker (Lexington, Mass.: Lexington Books, 1978), p. 211.

21. Kanowitz, *Women and the Law*, op. cit., p. 169; and Karen De Crow, *Sexist Justice* (New York: Vintage Books, 1975), pp. 243–45.

22. Cesare Lombroso and William Ferrero, *The Female Offender* (New York: D. Appleton, 1920), p. 152.

23. Ibid., pp. 150, 152, and 205.

24. Sigmund Freud, *New Introductory Lectures on Psychoanalysis* (New York: W. W. Norton, 1933), pp. 153–85.

25. Otto Pollak, *The Criminality of Women* (Philadelphia: University of Pennsylvania Press, 1950), p. 149.

26. Barbara Welter, "The Cult of True Womanhood: 1820–1860," in *Our American Sisters: Women in American Life and Thought*, ed. Jean E. Friedman and William G. Shade (Boston: Allyn and Bacon, 1973), pp. 96–115; William H. Chafe, *The American Woman: Her Changing Social, Economic, and Political Role, 1920–1970* (New York: Oxford University Press, 1972), pp. 199–225; and Robert W. Smuts, *Women and Work in America* (New York: Schocken, 1971), pp. 110–55.

27. Ibid.

28. Chafe, op. cit., pp. 135–73; and Smuts, op. cit., pp. 146–47.

29. Quoted in Chafe, op. cit., p. 176.

30. Ibid.

31. Ibid., pp. 226–44.

— *Two*—

WOMEN CRIMINALS IN THE CRIMINAL JUSTICE SYSTEM

Although the madonna/whore duality is easily seen in past cultures where one has the advantages of distance and hindsight, it is less obvious in modern society. Two of its embodiments are especially important for understanding the position of women in the criminal justice system. The first is the theory that attempts to link a change in female criminality with the present-day women's movement. Put in terms of Chapter 1, this theory argues that movements that help break down traditional roles make it more likely that women will deviate from the old norms and become whores. The second is the generally held view that the treatment of female criminals has been governed to some degree by a form of chivalry: the criminal justice system has tried to shield women in order to help the whores become madonnas and to ensure that the madonnas do not fall from grace. Both viewpoints have had the effect of channeling attention away from examining how the daily realities of life may be influencing female criminality. A similar tendency not to distinguish image from reality also permeates the prison system where women criminals are sent for punishment and rehabilitation.

The changes of the past two decades that have contributed to the increased participation, if not full acceptance, of women professionals in the criminal justice system, and to the overturning of laws such as the Muncy Act, also have been associated by many persons with a perceived alteration in the nature of crimes committed by women. Several researchers have argued that both the nature and extent of female criminality have changed; for example, women's criminal activity is increasing in all areas at a faster rate than men's; that women are committing more violent crimes than before; and that women are becoming more masculine in the kinds of crimes they commit and their methods. Researchers disagree on the precise nature of these changes, but there seems to be a consensus that they are somehow related to the women's movement of the 1960s. Since these theories have received much publicity, and since if proved to be true they will have wide implications for women in the criminal justice system, they must be examined carefully and with regard for the best available evidence.

EXTENT AND NATURE OF FEMALE CRIMINALITY

The impression that there has been an extraordinary increase in women's criminal activity since 1960 stems from a reading of the statistics presented in the standard source for gauging criminal activity in the United States, the Uniform Crime Reports, which have been published since 1930 by the Federal Bureau of Investigation. According to this source, from 1960 to 1975 the number of women arrested increased by 101.7 percent, and the number of men arrested during the same period increased by only 22.8 percent.[1] This includes arrests of females both over and under age 18. If the females under 18 are subtracted, there was an increase of 66.2 percent in the arrests of women from 1960 to 1975, and an increase of 6 percent from 1975 to 1977.[2] These numbers are somewhat misleading, since the percentage of arrests for women out of the total number of reported arrests for both men and women increased only from 10.7 percent to 15.7 percent, or about 5 percent, from 1960 to 1975.[3]

Actual numbers are more meaningful. A comparison of the number of men and women over 18 arrested during the period 1960–77 is as follows:[4]

	Men	Women
1960	2,665,044	304,165
1975	2,847,612	505,673
1977	2,930,027	536,132

In terms of total numbers, the increase in number of women arrested is not as great as one might be led to believe.

The question of whether or not women are now committing more violent and masculine types of crimes than before also can be judged by referring to the statistics. The Uniform Crime Reports are divided into two parts. Part I, entitled the Crime Index, presents a listing of those crimes that are considered as most representative of the trend of criminal activity across the country: the violent crimes of murder, forcible rape, robbery, aggravated assault, and the property crimes of burglary, larceny/theft, and motor vehicle theft (forcible rape is excluded in discussing women's criminality). Part II, which has no title of its own, lists all other crimes, including other assaults, fraud, embezzlement, prostitution and vice, narcotics offenses, gambling, drunken driving, drunkenness, disorderly conduct, vagrancy, loitering, and offenses relating to juveniles.[5]

From 1960 to 1975 the percentage of women arrested for part I crimes almost doubled, rising from 15.9 percent to 29.4 percent.[6] By itself this figure seems to portend an ominous trend. But of all women arrested during that period, only one-third commited part I crimes, whereas two-thirds committed part II crimes. Again, the actual numbers will be more meaningful. Table 2.1 lists, according to frequency, the ten leading crimes for which women over 18 were arrested from 1960 to 1977.

In the order of arrests, only larceny/theft and aggravated assault are part I crimes; the others are part II crimes. The increase in arrests for part I crime is due primarily to larceny/theft, a crime traditionally associated with women. In fact, an overall view of the criminal pattern of women since 1960 proves that the reasons for arrest have remained similar, with only fraud and drug offenses new to the list of the top ten crimes in 1975 and 1977.

The relative stability in the nature of female arrests is noteworthy when it is borne in mind that certain biases in the federal data should serve to exaggerate changes in the patterns of female criminality. For example, the Uniform Crime Reports are not adjusted according to the number of women in the population, demographic shifts, or major events, such as war, that temporarily remove large numbers of people from the general population. Women born in the baby boom of the late 1940s and early 1950s became members of the criminal age of risk, that is, 15 to 30 years, in the 1960s and 1970s. A rise in the number of women arrested may reflect this increase. Again, during the period 1960–77, there was a constant shift in population from rural to urban. Urban law enforcement agencies tend to be better equipped to record and submit arrest data than rural areas, and this may affect crime statistics. At the same time, the Vietnam War removed many men of the age of risk from the community, although the exact impact of this upon criminal statistics is impossible to estimate.[7]

Other changes have occurred in the areas of manpower and equipment, especially since the passage of the Omnibus Crime Control and Safe Streets Act of 1968. This act created the Law Enforcement

TABLE 2.1: RANK ORDER OF TEN LEADING CAUSES OF ARRESTS FOR WOMEN OVER 18 YEARS FOR YEARS 1960, 1975, and 1977.

1960: Total number of women over 18 arrested: 304,165

Drunkenness   102,698
Disorderly conduct   47,321
Larceny/theft   19,281
Prostitution/commercialized vice   17,943
Other assaults   11,125
Liquor laws   10,574
Gambling   9,948
Vagrancy   9,858
Driving under the influence   8,963
Aggravated assault   7,176

1975: Total number of women over 18 arrested: 505,673

Larceny/theft   109,856
Disorderly conduct   70,506
Drunkenness   45,984
Driving under the influence   34,129
Narcotic drug laws   30,827
Prostitution/commercialized vice   30, 274
Fraud   29,184
Other assaults   21,289
Aggravated assaults   13,546
Forgery/counterfeiting   9,292

1977: Total number of women over 18 arrested: 536,132

Larceny/theft   121,448
Disorderly conduct   52,908
Drunkenness   42,604
Driving under the influence   42,063
Prostitution/commercialized vice   34,466
Drug abuse violations   34,173
Other assaults   22,269
Fraud   19,106
Liquor laws   11,909
Aggravated assault   11,590

Sources: Federal Bureau of Investigation, *Uniform Crimes Reports,* 1976 and 1978. (Washington D.C.: Department of Justice) 1976, p. 183, and 1978, p. 175.

Assistance Administration (LEAA) in the Department of Justice to serve as that department's funding arm, providing money to law enforcement agencies for the addition of personnel and detection and data collection equipment. Apprehension and data-processing methods have been further improved with the use of computers and the addition of mobile patrol and communication units. This has had an undoubted influence on the number of arrests and the manner in which arrests have been recorded. It has provided many agencies with the resources to begin to record arrests for women separately from men. In those agencies that had no separate listings, any data starting with a base figure of zero resulted in a large percentage increase.[8]

Federal and state legislation and policies have created new kinds of crime, some of which are especially associated with women. Welfare fraud has become a new means for women to commit fraud, and in 1976 accounted for 34 percent of all women arrested for fraud.[9] Technological innovations, such as credit cards and computer banking, have added more opportunities for crime in the private sector, as have changes in the nature of retail outlets from small, owner-operated stores to large, impersonal department stores and supermarkets.

Finally, victims of crimes by women seem more willing than in the past to report these crimes to the authorities. This is especially true for shoplifting and employee theft. Law enforcement agencies, responding to increased pressure from victims, are taking a more aggressive role in arresting women offenders.[10]

Therefore, the rise that has occurred since 1960 in the incidence of crimes by women, from roughly 10 percent to 15 percent, can be explained largely on the basis of factors such as shifts in demography, improved enforcement, a greater willingness to arrest women, and so forth. Moreover, most of the changes in the various categories of crimes, as listed in the *Uniform Crime Reports*, are increases in those crimes traditionally associated with women. There does not seem to have been any great increase either in the incidence of female criminality or in the violence or aggressiveness of criminal activity.

CAUSAL LINK: CRIMINALITY AND THE WOMEN'S MOVEMENT

It may seem strange that researchers have argued that an increase in female criminality is one result of the women's movement. Since a change in the extent and nature of women's criminality is not borne out by statistics, it must rest on some preconceived idea about the impact of the women's movement on modern society.

This is true, for example, of the work of Freda Adler, who sees the women's movement as having eroded the defined "gender roles." The result is "the masculinization of female behavior," leading to a substantial increase in the rate of female criminality, including violent crimes.[11] Referring to the *Uniform Crime Reports*, she writes: "By every indicator available, female criminals appear to be surpassing males in the rate of increase for every major crime."[12]

However, statistics in the *Uniform Crime Reports* show that from 1960 to 1977 the only major part I offense for which women have outdistanced men is larceny/theft, the traditional women's crime. In fact, the increase in the number of women arrested for part I offenses during those years is due almost entirely to the increase in larceny/theft arrests. Furthermore, during this period women's rate of arrests for violent crimes remained stable, and no significant increase occurred in the other part I property crimes.[13] From the data it seems that women are not becoming criminals at a faster rate than men, nor are they becoming more violent or more masculinized in either their crimes or their methods.

Adler also attempts to link the women's movement with crimes of terrorism, under the assumption that in a traditionally male activity a woman participant is a member of the women's movement or influenced by the movement, or that the act of an individual woman signifies a trend for female criminality in general.[14] This part of her theory is not susceptible to statistical treatment since the data do not exist, but a case can be made against it on logical and historical grounds.

Women always have been involved in movements (political, economic, or social) that use the tools available at the moment. Participation by a woman is not a denial of womanhood; as the ex-slave and abolitionist Sojourner Truth said in 1851: "Look at my arm! I have ploughed and planted and gathered into barns, and no man could head me—and ain't I a woman? I could work as much and eat as much as a man—when I could get it—and bear the lash as well! And ain't I a woman?"[15] Similarly, a woman terrorist or, for that matter, a woman judge, may perceive herself as a traditional woman except for her terrorist activity or her judicial duties. History is full of examples of such women, among them Sarah Drummond, Sarah Grendon, and Lydia Chessman, participants in Bacon's Rebellion in Virginia in the seventeenth century; Margaret Corbin, Mary Hays and the Daughters of Liberty in the American Revolution in the eighteenth century; Sarah Grimke and Sojourner Truth, leaders in the antislavery movement in the nineteenth century; and the social and political reformers Emma Goldman and Elizabeth G. Flynn in the twentieth century.[16] Clearly, participation by women in various movements, even those involving terrorism, is not a new phenomenon, and that participation does not prove that women see themselves as being in any way less feminine.

The link between the women's movement and female criminality also is postulated by Rita Simon. According to her, women's participation in property crime "will increase as... employment opportunities expand and as... interests, desires, and definitions of self shift from a more traditional to a more liberated view."[17] As women's economic opportunities expand, owing to the women's movement, "their feelings of being victimized and exploited will decrease and their motivation to kill become muted."[18] Referring to the Uniform Crime Reports from 1953 to 1972, Simon writes: "The most striking change is in the arrests for larceny."[19] She notes that the percentage for criminal homicide "remained remarkably stable over the past 20 years...."[20]

Simon does not prove her fundamental premise, that women's economic opportunities have expanded in areas that would provide the opportunity for committing property crimes. In fact, the property crimes that have produced the largest increase in women's arrests are larceny/theft and fraud, both of which represent petty, unsophisticated crimes of low reward. Larceny, as a category in the Uniform Crime Reports, includes shoplifting, pickpocketing, purse snatching, and thefts without the use of force.[21] Studies done in the 1970s report that the overwhelming number of women arrested for larceny were shoplifting.[22] Fraud includes welfare fraud, passing bad checks, and credit card fraud.[23] The tables Simon refers to list fraud together with embezzlement, which makes it impossible to determine the number of women arrested for each. However, the 1975 Uniform Crime Reports lists fraud alone and does not mention embezzlement. The number of women over 18 arrested for fraud increased from 4,490 in 1960 to 29,184 in 1975; from the twelfth most frequent to the seventh for arrests of women.[24] Embezzlement was listed separately in the 1977 Uniform Crime Reports. The number of women over 18 arrested in 1968 was 746, and the number decreased to 697 in 1977. However, fraud arrests went from 9,481 in 1968 to 29,043 in 1977.[25]

Even embezzlement arrests cannot prove a link between economic opportunity for women and the incidence of crime. Embezzlement is sometimes associated with persons of high status and employment, but recent studies indicate that most arrests for embezzlement involve employees of low status and salary. Upper-level employees who embezzle are rarely reported to the police.[26]

Larceny, fraud, and embezzlement are hardly indicators of expanded economic opportunity, but in any case there is little evidence that women's economic opportunities have improved. Reports from the Bureau of Labor Statistics, economists, and private foundations suggest that women's economic situation actually has deteriorated since 1960. In 1978, 42 percent of women (42.1 million) over 16 years of age worked, an increase of 24.1 million women since 1960. This might suggest that the women's movement is having some impact on employment patterns, but in fact 80 percent of working women are in traditional low paying jobs: they make up 70 percent of clericals, 98 percent of domestics, and 55 percent of service employees. According to the Bureau of the Census, the gap in earnings between men and women has increased. Women earned 63 percent of what men earned on the average in 1955, but only 58 percent in 1977. In 1974 the median yearly earnings for men was $12,152 and for women $6,957; in 1977 the medians were $15,070 and $8,814.[27]

Because women were one of the last large groups to enter the labor market since 1960, they are at entry-level jobs and do not have seniority. Therefore, they are the first to be fired during any economic crunch. The Bureau of Labor Statistics in 1975 reported that 800,000 working women lost their jobs during the recessionary period of 1974–75. In February 1975, the percentage of white women unemployed was 7.6 percent, an increase from 4.7 percent in February 1974; black women had an unemployment rate of 10.9 percent, an increase from 7.9 percent in February 1974. Finally, women are heads of households of an increasing number of families below the poverty level.[28]

The figures demonstrate that women's criminal activity cannot have changed according to improved economic circumstances because for women no such improvement has occurred. The property crimes of larceny and fraud that are the major reason for the increase in incidence of arrest for women do not suggest economic improvement but rather the opposite: they confirm that women criminals now, as before, tend to commit certain kinds of relatively petty crimes of the sort one would expect from an economically disadvantaged group. Invariably, such women come mainly from certain ethnic groups that have had less than their share of social and economic opportunities.

Regardless of the source used, descriptions of women criminals have remained similar for the past 200 years. They have been from the lower socioeconomic class and usually from racial or religious minority groups. Lacking educational and vocational skills, they have been under-employed, if not unemployed. They have been arrested, convicted, and incarcerated for prostitution, drunkenness, disorderly conduct, vagrancy, larceny, fraud, and homicide against a member of the family or a friend.[29]

There certainly is evidence that women who cannot find jobs to support themselves and their families sometimes become criminals. Reports from women's reform organizations from the nineteenth century to the present have noted consistently that most women criminals were poor and needed employment; social commentators generally have agreed with this observation. Police records in New York City during the two world wars, the two high points of female employment, show a definite decrease in the incidence of property crimes by women. To this degree it is valid to say that women who do not follow the traditional roles and work are less likely to commit antisocial acts.[30]

But as is obvious from those who work with women criminals, they are not part of the women's movement, nor do their crimes reflect any involvement with the movement. Margery Velimeses, executive director of a program for female offenders in Philadelphia, writes: "A background of poverty [is] typical of incarcerated females."[31] The women she works with are school dropouts, unskilled, and working in low paying jobs if they work at all. Many of them steal because they must support a drug habit. Judy Hansen, director of a program in Pittsburgh, writes, "As the drug culture grows, as the country's economic situation deteriorates, and as the lot of the poor worsens, crime rates will continue to spiral."[32] Judy Glass, since 1975 a counsellor for women offenders at the Fortune Society (an organization in New York City dedicated to improving the conditions in jails and prisons and to helping ex-offenders readjust successfully in the community), does not think more women are committing crimes, but that more are being arrested:

> 75% of the women who come here from state prison were there for drug busts. Before the Rockefeller drug law, they would have gotten probation or a lesser charge. Also there is a great increase in women being prosecuted for welfare fraud. We are being prosecuted now for things that used to be dealt with by restitution or probation. Now there's jail.[33]

Glass also does not see any relationship between these women criminals and the women's movement. As one of the ex-offenders who did time in the women's jail on Rikers Island in New York City, she observed:

> From my experience, street women don't even relate to the women's movement that much. We think of it as a housewives' thing. We've always been liberated and we've always been considered to be aggressive. I doubt that more women are becoming aggressive because of the women's movement. I think poverty, poor education, or the lack of skills is more responsible.[34]

These remarks demonstrate how women criminals tend to mirror the attitudes of U.S. women in general. In 1975 Barbara Bryant, surveying 1,522 women across the country, found that only 30 percent were nontraditional in their view of marriage and employment; the other 70 percent, the traditionalists, believed that men should be the prime or sole supporters of their families.[35] Interestingly, the role-playing implicit in the traditionalist view is very evident in much female criminality. Women are not usually welcomed by men in the participation of crimes, and they are rarely leaders in crime. One study of men and women arrested for committing crimes together noted that the women were invariably the accessories; they were the wives and lovers, but the men made the plans. Women acting alone tend to commit the traditional women's crimes of larceny and prostitution, even if they have had some prior experience acting in concert with men as participants in burglaries or robberies.[36]

Women are not trusted by male thieves, who see them as emotional, weak, and unreliable. They are not brought into the "old boys" network of criminals and usually do not belong to gangs. A study of male fences and thieves in Pennsylvania found that the fences classed women with drug addicts and inexperienced thieves as people not to be trusted.[37]

In both the criminal and noncriminal populations of women there is a strong tendency to follow the traditional womanly roles, and a correspondingly small percentage of women seek to follow other roles. In the noncriminal world the nontraditionalists are usually white, middle class, well educated, and career oriented, just the kind of women who are seldom involved in crime and rarely arrested. Among women offenders, who are usually of the lower class, the values of the women's movement seem to have gotten no more hold than among U.S. women in general. There can be little doubt that the women's movement has had virtually no direct influence on female criminality during the past 20 years.

QUESTIONING CHIVALRY IN THE CRIMINAL JUSTICE SYSTEM

The realities of life that have helped shape the nature and extent of criminality by women often are overshadowed by concern with extraneous factors. The supposed drastic rise in the incidence of female crimes, in their violent and aggressive nature, and the links with the women's movement are theories that are not borne out by the evidence. Another view is that women benefit from a form of male chivalry practiced by members of the criminal justice system.

Chivalry has been cited by some researchers and workers to explain why women constitute so small a portion of the convicted criminals in the United States. In 1975 only 15.7 percent of all arrests were of women; 5.9 percent of all jail inmates and 3.4 percent of state and federal prison inmates were women. Chivalry means that women must be protected by men because they are weak and dependent. Because of this chivalrous attitude, it is argued, the criminal justice system treats women differently, and to their advantage, from men.[38]

Studies done in the 1960s to gauge the importance of chivalry are divided in their findings and suggest that arrests and sentencings of women are influenced by many factors. Some studies have concluded that if women conformed to stereotypical behavior by crying, showing deference to police, or concern for their children, they were less likely to be arrested.[39] Other studies found that police responded in a similar manner to the demeanor of men and women. They were less likely to arrest men or women who were polite, respectful, did not resist, and, most important, had not committed a violent crime. A study by Moyer and White of police in a southeastern city also confirmed that demeanor and type of offense, not the sex of the offender, influenced the decision of the police. Police officers admitted that if the offense was not serious, the main factor influencing their behavior was the attitude of the person arrested, whether male or female. Persons who "bad mouthed" the officers were more likely to be arrested. Thus the officers admitted to exercising considerable discretion when making arrests.[40]

Often, however, police discretion is affected by public policy of a formal or informal nature. For example, in the 1970s police officers in New York City tended not to arrest prostitutes because official priorities focused on more serious crimes in the cities. However, when the Democratic National Convention was held in the city in 1976, police were instructed to pick up all prostitutes in the convention area. Another example of the influence of policy is arrests for marijuana smoking. Increased use by middle- and upper-class persons and pressure for decriminalization led to decisions not to arrest. This was particularly true in areas where the penalty was severe, as in New York under the 1973 Rockefeller drug law.[41]

In the case of shoplifting, the low arrest rate before 1960 for women may have been the result of decisions by shopowners not to prosecute, on the rationale that it did not pay to go through the trouble of court expenses if the stolen merchandise was recovered when the woman was apprehended. In addition, the value of the item stolen probably determines whether or not the woman is reported to the police for arrest. Studies indicate that store administrators are more likely to call for the arrest of a person, man or woman, if the item is expensive. Men are more likely to be involved with high risk thefts than women, which probably explains why fewer women have been arrested in the past.[42]

On the other hand, there is evidence in recent years of a get-tough policy by store managers and owners. Since 1960 the arrests for shoplifting have increased so much that this crime has become the number one offense for which women are now being arrested. Perhaps the image presented in the news media of more aggressive, masculinized women criminals has prompted storeowners to treat crime by women in the same manner as by men. Whereas in previous years women caught shoplifting were released without arrest if the merchandise was returned immediately, now there is a greater willingness to call the police. Only in dealings with shoplifters of financial means, and usually Caucasian, do storeowners still exercise some of the old reluctance to involve the authorities.[43]

In another area of crime, employee thefts from businesses and corporations, there also is little clear evidence to support the chivalry theory. Some researchers have argued that chivalry is applied selectively to white women in high status positions. On the whole, however, it seems that arrests of employees for theft tend to involve both men and women without discrimination, with lower status employees much more likely to be arrested than higher status ones. The highest officers of business concerns are rarely ever arrested for theft.[44]

There is a generally held belief that a woman convicted of a crime is likely to receive probation if she is a mother. It could be argued that the real cause is money, for few states allow a mother to take her child into prison with her and it is expensive for the state to supply child care while the mother is incarcerated. But both arguments are beside the point, since approximately 75 percent to 90 percent of incarcerated women are mothers. Probation is thus not strongly influenced by motherhood, but probably by other factors such as the nature of the offense, prior criminal history, and family situation of the criminal.[45]

It is possible to cite still other reasons to explain why women may receive different treatment than male offenders. A less severe sentence may reflect the fact that women charged with part I property crimes other than larceny/theft usually are accessories, committing the crime upon the instructions of husbands or boyfriends. These same women, when acting alone, usually commit larceny/theft, which is not violent in nature. Women who commit the part I violent crimes, homicide or aggravated assault, usually do so spontaneously in their homes, against people known to them, often in reaction to being beaten. Because the violent crimes usually are not premeditated, nor committed during another crime, the women may be more likely to receive probation or lesser sentences than men who commit similar offenses.[46]

In another twist on the chivalry argument, Stuart Nagel and Lenore Weitzman reported in 1971 that sentencing depended on the type of crime committed. Those convicted of crimes traditionally associated with women received probation or suspended sentences, whereas those convicted of nontraditional crimes were incarcerated. These conclusions have been challenged by several recent studies that report no difference in sentencing between men and women of similar criminal backgrounds.[47]

Finally, a woman's race and social class may determine her sentence. The few white middle- and upper-class women who are arrested and convicted are likely to receive probation. The Manhattan Bail Project, conducted by the Vera Institute of Justice in New York City in 1962, reported that women released on bail while awaiting trial are less likely to be convicted than women awaiting trial in jail, and if convicted are less likely to be incarcerated. Minority women tend to be poor and have little or no support from family and community to help convince the judge to release them on bail. The result is that these women are disproportionately represented among incarcerated women. This is in keeping with the differential treatment afforded white middle- and upper-class women by the victims of crimes, by law enforcement officers, and by the courts.[48]

It appears that the theory of chivalry has little support in the evidence, and that the reality of arrest, trial, and punishment involves many factors. In fact, some researchers have argued quite the reverse of chivalry, that women are selectively discriminated *against* by the criminal justice system. Mention has been made in Chapter 1 of the state laws that mandated longer sentences for women than for men convicted of the same crimes. Carolyn Temin reports that despite the Daniel case, there still exists in Pennsylvania and other states laws providing for longer indeterminate sentences for women. Certainly discrimination is true of arrests and convictions for prostitution, which account for an estimated 30 to 50 percent of all incarcerated women.[49]

If chivalry does operate, it does so in ways that have been impossible to document conclusively, and without the consistency one would expect. Chivalry, like the link with the women's movement, seems to be an impressionistic theory in search of evidence, not a substantive issue in the understanding of the treatment of women in the criminal justice system.

INCARCERATED WOMEN

In examining the question of chivalry and the supposed link between female criminality and the women's movement, it has become evident that the traditional views of women and their roles have retained a great influence over the criminal justice system, and that as a result many of the realities of female criminality have been given insufficient attention. Unfortunately, this is true also for the treatment of female criminals once they have been sentenced and enter prison life. Here too the old stereotypes of how women behave and, even more important, how they ought to behave, have served only to obscure the realities. As a result, prisons have largely failed in their attempts to help "fallen" women attain respectability in the outside world.

Most of the studies concerning incarcerated women have been conducted since 1960, the overwhelming number since 1970. National interest in the criminal justice system, and corrections in particular, started in the 1960s and reached its peak after the Attica prison riot in September 1971. In 1965 President Lyndon B. Johnson issued Executive Order 11,236, which established the Commission on Law Enforcement and Administration of Justice. The commission presented its report, *The Challenge of Crime in a Free Society*, in February 1967. The report made more than 200 recommendations to control criminal behavior and called for "a greatly increased effort on the part of the Federal Government, the states, the counties, the cities, civic organizations, religious institutions, business groups and individual citizens."[50]

Following the publication of the commission's report, Congress passed the Omnibus Crime Control and Safe Streets Act in 1968, establishing a funding agency within the Department of Justice, the Law Enforcement Assistance Administration, for the purpose of providing money to law enforcement agencies for crime control purposes. In 1969 the Joint Commission on Correctional Manpower and Training recommended that money be appropriated for the purpose of training and finding employment for ex-offenders as a means of reducing recidivism. Subsequent studies emerged as government, professional, and private groups investigated the problems of crime and corrections.[51]

The reports issued by the federal government failed to recognize the needs of women inmates and ex-offenders; indeed, *The Challenge of Crime in a Free Society* did not even mention women. However, the efforts of women's organizations succeeded in prying some money from LEAA and other government agencies to fund research and programs for women inmates and ex-offenders.

One of the most recent of these reports, published in 1977, is by Ruth Glick and Virginia Neto. They studied selected prisons and jails in 14 states that held 6,466 women prisoners. The researchers reported that two-thirds of the women were under 35 years of age, the largest number falling between 22 and 25. Over half were black. Only 20 percent were married, but 75 percent had one child or more. Over half the women were on welfare prior to incarceration. If the women worked, the jobs were clerical, domestic service, or other types of unskilled, low paying work. Less than 60 percent had graduated from high school and 15 percent had only an elementary school education. Most of the women had a prior arrest history, one-third having been in juvenile facilities.[52]

The kinds of offenses for which women are incarcerated differ little among the various types of institutions. Studies conducted by the Federal Bureau of Prisons in 1973 and 1975 have produced a picture similar to that in a study done by the Women's Prison Association of New York City in 1972. In New York City the women had been imprisoned for a wide variety of offenses, including misdemeanors and felonies involving property, drugs, and violent crimes. In the federal prisons the women were convicted mostly of drugs, larceny/theft, and forgery. In general, women in all the studies were incarcerated most commonly for drugs and larceny/theft.[53]

According to Federal Bureau of Prison statistics, as of August 2, 1979, there were 1,482 women prisoners in seven federal institutions. Two prisons were exclusively for women, Alderson (West Virginia) and Pleasanton (California); two were cocorrectional, Fort Worth (Texas) and Lexington (Kentucky); and three were detention centers, metropolitan correctional centers in New York City, Chicago, and San Diego.[54]

Regarding institutions outside the federal system, statistics are available from the Bureau of the Census for both jails and prisons. As of February 15, 1978, there were ten jails exclusively for women, located in large cities such as Chicago, Los Angeles, and New York. Out of a total jail population of 158,394, there were 9,555 females, of whom 278 were juveniles. During March 1979 the average daily population of prisons was 9,836 females out of a total of 268,382 prisoners (which includes about 8,000 persons in community-based corrections). The number of prisons only for women was 46 as of March 1979, the large number due to the fact that several states have more than one institution called by the term "prison." North Carolina, for example, has five such prisons where it sends women sentenced to more than 90 days. In states that have no separate jails or prisons for women, they are housed in sections of male facilities. Eight states contract with neighboring states to board out their women convicts; women sentenced to over two years in Hawaii are sent to the women's prison in California.[55]

Institutions for men only and for both men and women are frequently located in or near urban areas, but those for women only are usually set in rural areas. This peculiarity is a result of ideas current in the nineteenth century, when the geographic location of most correctional institutions was determined. Women reformers believed that women criminals could be saved only if they were removed from the corrupting influences of cities and men. Prisons were therefore set in the countryside and staffed with women only.[56]

Since women criminals were perceived as being potential madonnas, that is, proper housewives, if only they could be rehabilitated, their prison regimen was designed to instill a sense of decency and homelife. This was established from the very beginning by the various reform groups that arose in the nineteenth century. They were run by upper- and middle-class women, who, because of their social background, perpetuated the concept of the traditional woman. In the early twentieth century, lawyer and prison reformer Madeleine Doty wrote: "Someday the thing I have dreamed must come true. Prisons will be transformed, changed from a prison to a home. At its head will be a wise, intelligent mother, able to distinguish between the daughter who would be a militant and the one who would be a Jane Austen, treating each according to her need."[57]

Following this ideal, women's prisons were, and usually are, small, with a normal capacity of under 250 inmates, and arranged with many cottages or housing units within walking distance of the dining room and other facilities. Often the inmates have their own rooms. When Sarah Smith, superintendent of the first women's prison, greeted the first inmate, Sallie Hubbard, in 1873, she "embraced her fallen sister," and after praying for her salvation took her to a room decorated with a bedspread, curtains, table with flowers, and a bible. It was a room, not a cell.[58] In the 1970s a superintendent of a women's jail remarked on the atmosphere, "We're a lot like a family here...this is home for most of them."[59]

Rarely are there signs of external security such as concrete walls, fences or gun turrets since these are medium or minimum security facilities. Except for those women classified as maximum security, the others are free to walk to and from their housing and other buildings. The purpose of this type of design is to create, as much as possible, a homelike atmosphere, with individual rooms decorated by the women in cottages or small buildings that would simulate a home where women would learn to be homemakers from the cottage officers.[60]

The openness of the prison and the relative freedom given to most inmates are understandable, considering the type of women sent to these prisons when they first opened at the end of the nineteenth century and early in the twentieth. Most of the women had convictions of prostitution, adultery, disorderly conduct, drunkenness, and stubbornness; few had convictions of property or violent crimes. For example, of the 640 women incarcerated from 1877–1913 whose records were studied at the prison in Massachusetts, 56.8 percent had convictions of offenses against public order, 26.8 percent of chastity offenses, 12.5 percent of property offenses, and 3.9 percent of violent offenses. They all served at least one year.[61] These were not dangerous or violent women who posed a threat to either the staff or the community. All they needed for their rehabilitation, according to the reformers, was the model of pious, moral women and teachers in a domestic setting out in the country.

No matter how idyllic the location, many problems were and continue to be posed for the inmates. Most of them come from cities, and since there is either only one women's facility in a state or none at all, and the women must be boarded out, it is impossible to place them in a facility near home. Because of the distance, and often the lack of public transportation, visits from friends and family are infrequent; this problem is most severe for women in federal facilities. As a result, it is difficult for the inmate to keep close ties with her family, her community, and even her lawyer; it becomes too expensive to make frequent phone calls. The problem becomes acute for women boarded out, such as those in Hawaii, sentenced for over two years, who are sent to California, 2,400 miles from home.[62]

The rural location, meant to remove women from corruption, also has removed them from schools, training programs, and jobs, usually found in cities, that could be taken advantage of on a work/study release program. If women do have the opportunity to study or work in the community where the prison is located, they cannot continue with this upon discharge from the prison because their homes are too far for them to commute; they must start anew.

Location in rural areas also leads to staffing problems. Women living in the area, usually white, take the jobs as correction officers because there are few jobs available in the community. Staff turnover is high and staff shortages common. (Often the institution, whether male or female, is the major source of employment and necessary to the economy of the community.) Women incarcerated in these institutions, especially in the large industrial and urban states, tend to be city women and members of minority groups. The differences in life-styles, race, and values create additional tensions between the prisoners and the staff.

The traditional attitudes implicit in the location of the prisons are carried over in the training programs designed to prepare inmates for life in the outside world. The emphasis is heavily on the womanly tasks that revolve about the home. Inmates prepare and serve meals, wash and iron clothes, clean, sew, and the like. These activities also contribute substantially to the daily needs of the institution; institutional needs are more important than the needs of the inmates for useful training. These institutional maintenance chores are referred to as vocational training programs for women. Nonmaintenance training programs also prepare women for traditional women's jobs, such as cosmetology, nurse's aide, typist, clerical work, and food services.

These programs may reduce the cost of maintaining the institution, but they rarely prepare the women for jobs in the outside world. In any case, many states have requirements for certain jobs. A licensed cosmetologist must have hundreds of hours of instruction and no felony convictions. A licensed nurse's aide cannot have a felony or a history of drug use. A typist must be able to read and spell correctly, but few incarcerated women, 67 percent of whom never graduated high school, are skilled to do anything but copy typing.

For many, prostitution pays more than a low-level typing job. In addition, most incarcerated women have a drug-use problem and many are addicted. Of the few addicts who are cured by imprisonment, most find their scars a hindrance to employment, especially in jobs such as waitressing that often require short-sleeved uniforms. In most cases, therefore, training women for traditional women's work is unrealistic if the goal is to make them self-supporting.

Proposals for nontraditional training for women face several obstacles. Most of these programs cost a great deal of money. Since in each state there is only one prison for women (or none at all), all classifications of women over the age of 16 are housed in the single facility. Therefore, the women are so diverse in their criminal backgrounds, employment and educational levels, and marital and family status that only a few would be qualified or willing to participate in these programs. Moreover, since the cost per woman can reach up to $20,000 a year, the additional cost to make these training programs available for the small number becomes formidable. Welding, carpentry, auto repair, printing, and electronics shops, available in many men's prisons for use by hundreds of inmates, are prohibitively expensive in women's institutions. Private industry, too, has been reluctant to invest in women inmates. For example, in 1975–76, the superintendent of the New York City Correctional Institution for Women could not get any private company to provide business machines and instructors to train the women because the cost per trainee would be too high.[63]

Furthermore, government funding agencies are more likely to grant money for traditional training than for nontraditional. In keeping with the attitudes toward women and their roles, typing is preferred to welding. There were two government-funded typing programs for the inmates at the New York City jail in 1975–76: one on a work/study release basis at the Women Prison Association's Hopper Home, called Open Door, and the other in the jail, developed by the New York Junior League and funded by the National Institute on Drug Abuse. However, owing to their limited educational experience, few women were able to learn to type correctly. Not one graduate of the typing courses could be placed in a job, even though both programs had job placement staff.[64]

There are so few nontraditional training programs that they stand out. A welding program at the Women's House of Corrections in Jessup, Maryland, has been sponsored by the Baltimore Council AFL-CIO since 1973. The number of women hired is related to the availability of jobs. Despite employment problems, this program has been successful in its effort to train women in skills that helped make them employable.[65]

Federal funds allocated through the Comprehensive Employment and Training Act (CETA) of 1974 are used by community and institutional training programs to train inmates and ex-offenders, although few women seem to benefit. The previously cited 1977 study by Glick and Neto reported that all prisons and almost every large jail had educational and vocational programs, but they were primarily in traditional women's skills; ironically, many programs trained women in skills that required licenses that were denied to ex-offenders. The researchers concluded that the small, poor offerings in training programs resulted from traditional views of the capacity and needs of women and the maintenance needs of the institution.[66]

The difficulty of ex-offenders in finding employment is exacerbated by their lack of skills and by the reluctance of employers to hire women in nontraditional jobs. Many government-funded employment services were established after 1968 for the purpose of finding employment for ex-offenders. One such agency was the National Alliance of Businessmen, which was organized in 1968 by presidential mandate. A representative of the Alliance in New York City reported that they did not even try to find jobs for women because it was impossible; men could be placed in jobs that required physical strength even if they had no specific skills, but women could not. Job placement staff in other agencies said that they usually could get clerical or typing jobs for women, but few women were qualified for those jobs. Given the cost of providing nontraditional training and the difficulty of finding jobs for women, government planners preparing budgets fall back on the unrealistic view of women in general and women inmates in particular, and continue to train for skills that are required to maintain the institution. They assume that women have men to support them.[67]

Vocational programs, even the traditional ones, rarely exist for women incarcerated in sections of male jails. Women are more restricted and idle in these facilities because they are not welcomed, and are seen as a security problem since they have to be kept separate from the men. Usually they are housed on one section or floor of the jail and are restricted to their self-contained housing areas all day, rarely leaving to have any exercise or recreation. Because there are so few in each of these jails, no classification exists and detained and sentenced women are often housed together.[68]

In addition to training in skills that prepare for a job, many of the women need training in skills that will prepare them to be mothers. Many women inmates have a history of being abused as children, and therefore have no positive mother-child experience. Incarcerated women who are pregnant need special medical care, as well as programs in family life, child rearing, and mothering. These programs are not readily available in all the prisons and jails for women.

Pregnant women have their babies in local hospitals, after which they return to the institution and the children are sent either to relatives or a foster home. As of 1974, prisons that had nurseries for infants included: Bedford Hills, New York; Muncy, Pennsylvania; and Raleigh, North Carolina. Since 1970, efforts have been made to reunite mothers with their infants and other children. The Purdy Treatment Center in Washington state, opened in 1970, allows children weekend visits with their mothers and unlimited visits during the week. the visits are encouraged to help prepare the women for family life and mothering and to maintain family relationships. There is also a preschool nursery program that children from the community attend four mornings a week and the inmates' children attend the fifth morning. The inmates are aides to certified teachers; working with children under supervision also teaches them to be better mothers to their own children.[69]

Several states have laws permitting women to have their children with them in prison, but most women, feeling that prison is no place for children, have not taken advantage of the opportunity. Most state legislatures argue against such programs and may even deny the mother custody of her children after she is released. In Washington, Wisconsin, Nebraska, Kentucky, and New Jersey there are programs permitting children to visit for weekends, but mother-child programs are not common. Currently there are two studies being conducted on the subject, both of which support permitting the mother to have her children with her.[70]

Two parenting programs started in 1978 in the women's prison in Clinton, New Jersey. Title XX, a federally funded program, provides for child visits. Clinton is in the center of the state in a rural, suburban area, whereas most of the women come from cities in the northern part of the state. this program provides transportation from all over the state to give the children of all inmates at least one visit a month. During the day-long visit, mothers and children eat together and spend time together in meeting rooms or nursery areas that were specially prepared with furniture and toys. Counselors and special service personnel provide guidance and assistance to help the mothers develop and maintain relationships with their children. In the other program, several selected women with minimum security status who are within a few months of being released from the prison are permitted to go to Camp Retreat with their children for a series of three weekends; family counseling is provided. The camp is owned by the Salvation Army, which also provides the funding and personnel. Since the programs have been in effect only since 1978, no conclusive results have been reported to indicate the impact on women and their children after the women go home. Program staff reported that morale improved among those women who participated, but the major problem with any of these programs is the lack of aftercare support once the women return home.[71]

Although mothering is in keeping with a woman's traditional role, incarcerated women are denied that relationship and may even have the children permanently taken from them as part of their punishment for crime. This may be done even though studies indicate that allowing women to perform their mothering role contributes to their rehabilitation and keeps families united. Approximately three-fourths of the women lived with their children prior to incarceration. Many do not see their children during their period of incarceration because of state laws, distance from their home, lack of transportation to the institution, and the lack of money and personnel to properly supervise family visits.[72]

The two most important needs of incarcerated women are jobs and family. A report on health care in correctional facilities listed other special needs of women: Pap smears, breast examinations, venereal disease tests, contraception and abortion information, pregnancy care and treatment for menstrual problems and anemia. Another concern is the separation trauma of the mother after birth. Women also require obstetrician-gynecologists, which few institutions hire on either a full- or part-time basis.[73]

Given the lack of any national standards, institutions respond individually to the image of womanhood and the need for special services or equipment. For example, in 1978 a new prison was built at Trenton, New Jersey; the only bathtub in the facility is located in the housing area for women because women are supposed to require baths for medical reasons. In the New York City Correctional Institution for Women, a schedule was arranged in 1975 for women to go to the clinic to have their legs shaved. Because razor blades are weapons, the women could not have them in their rooms, but at least their grooming needs were recognized. It is common for women in prisons to wear jewelry and use makeup; these also are considered women's needs. On the other hand, some very important needs are not met, the rationale being that they are not womanly. There is a tendency for women in prisons and jails to gain weight from the starchy food, candy, and other snacks bought in the commissary, and because of the lack of exercise. However, athletic activities, sports, and exercise classes generally are not available in most women's facilities.[74]

THE FUTURE

On the whole, the picture of life in women's prisons is not encouraging. The innovative programs in training, mothering, and health care are conspicuous precisely because they are so few. What is remarkable is how little has changed during the past 100 years. Since the first prison for women opened in 1873, some changes have occurred, but the basic premises have remained the same. Both in and out of prison, women tend to be treated according to the traditional view, that is, as wives and mothers. Women criminals are disgraced and dishonored women who must be punished but who can be reformed by good women.

Given these entrenched values, it is unlikely that prison programs will change much in the future. Equally important is the economic situation of the 1970s which has made any increases in funds for women's corrections unlikely. Recession, inflation, and unemployment, as well as the Proposition 13 tax-cut mentality, are reducing government budgets. Citizens who are unemployed or who feel the economic pinch in some other way will resent any tax money spent on "making life easy" for prisoners or on training programs and on-job counseling; prisoners should be punished, not pampered. Tax cuts force budget cuts, and the corrections system, always the least well-funded part of the criminal justice system, will have to eliminate "unessential" services and programs.

Nor is there much hope at the other end of the problem: the incidence of female criminality. Unless there is an extraordinary change in the patterns of economic, racial, and sexual discrimination, criminal behavior among women will continue along the same lines. As long as women face high unemployment, a limited range of jobs, and few well-paying jobs, they will constitute a large group at or below the poverty level. Those who become dependent on drugs or alcohol will be caught in an especially vicious bind, since their addiction will reduce their ability to work and will make petty crime, especially theft and prostitution, the most viable livelihood.

The only slim hope for a reduction in criminal activity is in demography, which is gradually reducing the number of women in the age of risk. The *Uniform Crime Reports* from 1975 to 1977 show that the crime rate may be leveling off. The population boom of the 1950s has peaked, and it is estimated that in 1990 there will be 1.3 million fewer young workers than in the mid-1970s. Unemployment rates among teenagers (35 percent in 1976) should decline, which should reduce the rate of property crimes, particularly larceny.[75]

Even if women's crime rate does not decrease significantly, other factors indicate that the rate will not increase appreciably and that criminal behavior will not alter from traditional patterns. Sex discrimination in the criminal world will keep women in their place. They will not become partners in crime, equal members of gangs, or be admitted to the "old boys" network. They will remain accessories or sex objects. Further, nontraditional crimes often require women to go on the streets alone at night, where, as women, they are vulnerable to rape in addition to robbery. This will limit the number of venturesome women.[76]

This of course, will not console the women who do commit crimes and suffer conviction and incarceration. They will leave the world and enter total obscurity. Although much publicity has been given to the woman criminal in the past decade, the woman prisoner is largely ignored. She does not riot, escape, commit suicide, or do violence to the staff and other inmates; she is out of sight and out of mind. Ironically, the publicity about women criminals has created an image of a more dangerous type of criminal who must be arrested more often and punished more harshly. But this image has as little evidence to substantiate it as does the theory of chivalry and the view that women must be rehabilitated by training them in household tasks and typing. Unfortunately, these images continue to mold perceptions and action by both the public and some professionals in the criminal justice system. In all this concern with theories, stereotypes and images, the human being behind the criminal mask has been forgotten.

NOTES

1. Federal Bureau of Investigation, *Uniform Crime Reports* (Washington, D.C.: Department of Justice, 1976), p. 183. (All following references to these reports will list only the name and year.)

2. *Uniform Crime Reports*, 1978, p. 175.

3. *Uniform Crime Reports*, 1976, p. 183.

4. *Uniform Crime Reports*, 1978, p. 175.

5. Ibid., pp. 6–7 and 183.

6. Ibid., p. 183.

7. Ibid., pp. 1–7; *Uniform Crime Reports*, 1976, pp. 1–5; and Laural L. Rans, "Women's Crime: Much Ado About...?" *Federal Probation*, March 1978, pp. 1–2 (reprint).

8. Ibid.

9. *ACLU News* (Washington, D.C.: National Prison Project, 1978), p. 3 (report for release, October 5, 1978).

10. Darrell J. Steffensmeier, "Sex Differences in Patterns of Adult Crime, 1965–77; A Review and Assessment" (Paper presented at the Annual Meeting of the National Institute of Crime and Delinquency, 1979), p. 21; and Meda Chesney-Lind, "Chivalry Reexamined: Women and the Criminal Justice System," in Lee H. Bowker, *Women, Crime, and the Criminal Justice System* (Lexington, Mass.: Lexington Books, 1978), pp. 201–2.

11. Freda Adler, *Sisters in Crime: The Rise of the New Female Criminal* (New York: McGraw-Hill, 1975), pp. 1–3.

12. Ibid., p. 15.

13. *Uniform Crime Reports*, 1976, p. 183; and *Uniform Crime Reports*, 1978, p. 175.

14. Adler, op. cit., pp. 20–21.

15. Eleanor Flexner, *Century of Struggle: The Woman's Rights Movement in the United States* (New York: Atheneum, 1971), p. 91.

16. Julia C. Spruill, *Women's Life and Work in the Southern Colonies* (New York: Norton Library, 1972), pp. 232–54; Emma Goldman, *Living My Life* (New York: New American Library, 1977); Elizabeth G. Flynn, *The Rebel Girl: An Autobiography, My First Life, 1906–1926* (New York: International Publishers, 1973); and Gerda Lerner, ed., *The Female Experience: An American Documentary* (Indianapolis: Bobbs-Merrill, 1977). These are a few references about women considered terrorists or revolutionaries in their day.

17. Rita J. Simon, *The Contemporary Woman and Crime* (Washington, D.C.: National Institute of Mental Health, 1975), p. 40.

18. Ibid., p. 4.

19. Ibid., pp. 41–42 and 44.

20. Ibid.

21. *Uniform Crime Reports*, 1978, p. 27.

22. Steffensmeier, op. cit., p. 17.

23. *Uniform Crime Reports*, 1976, p. 6.

24. Ibid., p. 183.

25. *Uniform Crime Reports*, 1978, p. 175.

26. Steffensmeier, op. cit., pp. 18–19; and Chesney-Lind, op. cit., p. 201.

27. Alan Pifer, *Women Working: Towards a New Society* (Reprinted from the 1976 Annual Report of the Carnegie Corporation of New York), pp. 3–12.; *New York Times*, February 19, 1977, p. 23; *Trenton Times*, November 29, 1976, p. A2; National Commission of Working Women, *An Overview of Women in the Workforce* (Washington, D.C.: National Commission of Working Women Center for Women and Work, 1978), pp. 1–2; and *ACLU News*, op. cit., pp. 2–4.

28. Ibid.

29. Clarice Feinman, "Imprisoned Women: A History of the Treatment of Women Incarcerated in New York City, 1932–1975" (Ph.D. diss., New York University, 1976) pp. 43, 50–51, and 150–52; *Female Offenders in the Federal Correctional System* (Washington, D.C.: United States Bureau of Prisons, undated), p. 4; Ruth M. Glick and Virginia V. Neto, *National Study of Women's Correctional Programs* (Washington, D.C.: National Institute of Law Enforcement and Criminal Justice, 1977), pp. xvii–xix; Women's Prison Association of New York City, *Annual Reports, 1915–43*; Estelle B. Freedman, "Their Sisters' Keepers: An Historical Perspective on Female Correctional Institutions in the United States: 1870–1900," *Feminist Studies* 2 (1974): 82–83; and Spruill, op. cit., pp. 314–39.

30. New York City Police Department, *Annual Report, 1917*, p. 26; *1920*, p. 312; *1930*, p. 170; *1940*, p. 112; and *1950*, p. 130.

31. Margery L. Velimesis, "The Female Offender," *Crime and Delinquency Literature* (March 1975): 94.

32. Judy P. Hansen, "Women's Rights, and Wrongs," *New York Times*, March 17, 1975, p. 29.

33. "Women, Prison and 'Getting Out'," *Fortune News*, April 1979, p. 5.

34. Ibid.

35. Barbara E. Bryant, *American Women Today and Tomorrow* (Washington, D.C.: National Commission of the Observance of International Women's Year, 1977), pp. 1–5.

36. Carol Lee Fenster, "Characteristics of Females Arrested with Males in Crime Partnerships" (Paper presented at the Western Social Science Association, 1977), pp. 13–14; and Steffensmeier, op. cit., pp. 28–31.

37. Steffensmeier, op. cit., and *New York Times*, March 6, 1978, pp. B1 and B8.

38. Laura Crites, "Women in the Criminal Court," in *Women in the Courts*, ed. Winifred L. Hepperle and Laura Crites (Williamsburg, Va.: National Center for State Courts, 1978), p. 168.

39. Chesney-Lind, op. cit., pp. 203 and 207.

40. Imogene L. Moyer and Garland F. White, "Police Processing of Female Offenders" (Paper presented at the Annual Meeting of the Academy of Criminal Justice Sciences, 1979), pp. 19–22.

41. *New York Times*, July 8, 1979, p. 34; and an interview with Essie O. Murph, former superintendent, New York City Correctional Institution for Women, June–December 1976.

42. Chesney-Lind, op. cit., pp. 199–201.

43. Ibid., p. 201; and Steffensmeier, op. cit., p. 23.

44. Chesney-Lind, op. cit., pp. 199–201; and Steffensmeier, op. cit., p. 23.

45. Crites, op. cit., p. 171.

46. Ibid., pp. 170–71.

47. Stuart Nagel and Lenore Weitzman, "Women as Litigants," *Hastings Law Review* 23 (1971): 171–181.

48. Clarice Feinman, "An Afro-American Experience: The Women in New York City's Jail," *Afro-Americans in New York Life and History* 1 (July 1977): 204.

49. Carolyn Temin, "Discriminatory Sentencing of Women Offenders," *American Criminal Law Review* 11 (1973): 357–69; *Sunday Bulletin*, November 27, 1977, p. 8; and Chesney-Lind, op. cit., pp. 203–7.

50. Commission of Law Enforcement and Administration of Justice, *The Challenge of Crime in a Free Society* (Washington, D.C.: United States Government Printing Office, 1967), p. v.

51. Lloyd E. Ohlin, ed. *Prisoners in America* (Englewood Cliffs, N.J.: Prentice-Hall, 1973), pp. 2 and 6–7.

52. Glick and Neto, op. cit., pp. xvii–xix and 102–56.

53. Ibid., pp. 141–56; *Female Offenders in the Federal Correctional System*, op. cit., p. 7; Omar Hendrix, *A Study in Neglect: A Report on Women Prisons* (New York: Women's Prison Association of New York City, 1972), pp. 16–18; and Federal Bureau of Prisons, "Federal Prisoners under Sentence and not under Sentence, Confined in Bureau of Prison's Institutions by Offence, Race, and Sex, June 30, 1975," printout from the Department of Justice, Table A-5.

54. Information from Mike Aun, Federal Bureau of Prisons, Department of Justice, August 1979.

55. Information from David Schaitberger, Bureau of Census, Department of Labor, August 1979.

56. Glick and Neto, op. cit., pp. 11–13; Hendrix, op. cit., p. 39; and Feinman, "Imprisoned Women," op. cit., pp. 42–45.

57. Madeleine A. Doty, *Society's Misfits* (New York: Century, 1916), p. 100.

58. Estelle Freedman, "Women's Prison Experience in Nineteenth Century America," (Paper presented at the 18th Annual National Archives Conference, 1978), p. 1.

59. Kathryn W. Burkhart, *Women in Prison* (New York: Doubleday, 1973), p. 127.

60. Glick and Neto, op. cit., pp. 20–28.

61. Freedman, "Women's Prison Experience," op. cit., fn. 4.

62. "The Sexual Segregation of American Prisons," *Yale Law Journal* 82 (May 1973): 1232–34.

63. Glick and Neto, op. cit., pp. 70–77; Feinman, "An Afro-American Experience," op. cit., pp. 204–7; and interview, Murph, op. cit.

64. Feinman, "Imprisoned Women," op. cit., pp. 268–71, and 284.

65. Virginia A. McArthur, *From Convict to Citizen: Programs for the Woman Offender* (Washington, D.C.: Government of the District of Columbia Commission on the Status of Women, 1974), pp. 14–15.

66. Glick and Neto, op. cit., pp. 70–77; and "The Sexual Segregation of American Prisons," op. cit., pp. 1241–43.

67. Hendrix, op. cit., pp. 39–40; and Feinman, "Imprisoned Women," op. cit., pp. 289–92.

68. Linda R. Singer, "Women and the Correctional Process," *American Criminal Law Review* 11 (1973): 299–302; "The Sexual Segregation of American Prisons," op. cit., pp. 1237–43; and Hendrix, op. cit., pp. 6–8, and 23–27.

69. Velimesis, op. cit., p. 102; and *Female Offenders: Problems and Programs* (Washington, D.C.: American Bar Association Female Offender Resource Center, 1976), pp. 26–27.

70. Phyllis Jo Baunach, "Effects of the Mother-Child Separation of Inmate-Mothers" (Paper presented at the Annual Meeting of the American Society of Criminology, 1978), pp. 15–17.

71. Interview, Sherry MacPhearson, Professional Services Department, Correctional Institution for Women, Clinton, New Jersey, May 3, 1979.

72. Ibid.; and Baunach, op. cit., pp. 4–7.

73. Edward M. Brecher and Richard D. Della Penna, *Health Care in Correctional Institutions* (Washington, D.C.: National Institute of Law Enforcement and Criminal Justice, 1975), pp. 33–35.

74. Ibid.; interview, Murph, op. cit.; and interview, Richard D. Della Penna, medical director, New York City Correctional Institution for Women, March 12, 1974.

75. Pifer, op. cit., p. 4.

76. Steffensmeier, op. cit., pp. 23–33.

— *Three* —

WOMEN IN CORRECTIONS

If the public has little regard for the inmates of prisons and jails, it has only slightly more for the correction officers who guard the inmates. Movies and television have created a stereotype of cruel and brutal male guards and sexually suspect female guards. Given the degree of general ignorance about correction officers, it is not surprising that women correction officers are the least known and understood of all women in the criminal justice system. Even social scientists have tended to concentrate on men, who make up most of the inmates and officers, to the detriment of the women.

In the 1970s, the ignorance and neglect began to diminish as women moved out of women-only institutions; in so doing they competed directly with men for positions in the system and asked for equality of pay and opportunity. Predictably, all the male stereotypes about women have surfaced in the ensuing debate. Yet, in a way, these women are only continuing the pattern set a century ago. It always has been women, not men, who have been the moving force in women's corrections, and who have established a viable role for women in the criminal justice system. Today's professionals are following that pattern.

HISTORICAL BACKGROUND

Women entered corrections as reformers in the nineteenth century, an age of growing social problems, rapid changes in the status and role of women, and enormous zeal for reform. The Women's Christian Temperance Union, the Moral Reform Society, and Women's Prison Association were among the organizations that tried to improve the lot of women and society. The reformers were ladies of the middle and upper classes who felt an obligation to be useful in society. They were part of a remarkable development in the roles of women. On the one hand the idea had arisen, and was to become especially strong in the Victorian era, that proper women were housewives and mothers only, and had no employment outside the home, not even as part of their husbands' businesses. These women were devoted to the "cult of true womanhood," with its emphasis on feminine subordination and passivity, except in a few areas such as community service. But from the mid-nineteenth century onward there also were significant numbers of women from the propertied classes who had acquired college educations and advanced and professional degrees. Many of these educated women entered employment as teachers, lawyers, social workers, settlement house workers, and the like, instead of becoming traditional housewives. Women of this sort, who lacked a clear position in either the home or the outside world, managed as best they could in an often hostile male world.[1]

Both groups, however, agreed on the need for certain kinds of reform affecting "fallen" women. One of the first goals was the eradication of prostitution, an offense that carried strong moral overtones. Prostitution was one obvious result of urbanization, industrialization, and immigration. Vast numbers of poor, uneducated women, especially immigrants, provided the cheap labor that powered U.S. business in the nineteenth century. Their lives were hard, and many discovered the quick and tangible rewards of selling their bodies. In doing so they violated all of the womanly ideals held sacred by the wealthier classes, and in general were regarded as destructive temptresses who sought the downfall of men. Here was a field ripe for reform.[2]

In 1834 a group of ladies formed the New York Female Moral Reform Society. From the very beginning they took the then novel view that the true blame for prostitution rested on the men, whom they accused of destroying innocent women to satisfy base desires. Society could be cleansed of prostitution mainly by controlling men's sexual behavior (which would also eliminate adultery) and by converting the prostitutes into good Protestants. The reformers, fired by the religious zeal of the Second Great Awakening, expressed "a strident hostility to the licentious and predatory male."[3]

Despite the strong moralistic tone of their program, the reformers also attacked some of the economic conditions that helped encourage prostitution. They proposed that women be given more economic opportunities, especially in areas then considered men's work; they encouraged the organization of unions to protect the rights of working women. Nevertheless, there was no attempt to make basic changes in either economy or society.[4]

This conservatism was typical of most women's reform movements of the nineteenth century. The wealth and position of the reformers made the movements traditional rather than militant. The reform programs usually were phrased in religious terms, and the prostitutes were "fallen" women whom the good and pious must "uplift." There also were some other elements of a more self-interested nature. Curbing prostitution, it was argued, would reduce the number of illegitimate births, and since most prostitutes were immigrants, a reduction in illegitimacy would lessen the increase of elements that threatened to "bastardize American civilization." Josephine Shaw Lowell, a patrician active in the development of women's corrections, regarded prostitutes "a serious eugenic danger to society" that had to be removed.[5] Thus the efforts against prostitution also carried class connotations.

It quickly became apparent that one part of the reform program, the reining in of male sexual desires, was not feasible. Reformers therefore concentrated in other areas, such as the rehabilitation of the fallen women. Since men were corrupters, they must be kept away from susceptible women, which meant that facilities for the raising up of prostitutes and other fallen women had to be strictly segregated from the male world. This view soon was established as a basic element of the reform movement, where it fit easily with the belief of proper women that, on the whole, women were the moral and spiritual superiors of men. The segregation of women in corrections therefore was justified on practical and theoretical grounds. The natural result was the creation of a prison system for women only, staffed by women; many reformers became professionals in corrections for women.

The U.S. penal system had, by the late eighteenth century, undergone a major change. Under the impetus of a fervent religious conviction, it was decided that the usual punishments for crimes, such as flogging, mutilation, and death, should be replaced by rehabilitation. Through religious instruction, meditation on past wrongs, and hard work, criminals could be made to see the evil of their ways and recant their antisocial views. Criminals thus reformed would be saved for both God and society.

At first women were not considered worthy or capable of benefiting from this new approach. Female offenders seemed especially depraved because they had deserted the proper womanly place and had done those things that only evil men were supposed to do. Since these men obviously were beyond redemption, little effort was made to help them and conditions in jails became atrocious. The lack of institutions specifically for women meant that females were incarcerated in wings, rooms, and attics of men's penitentiaries, separated from the male inmates but supervised by male guards. All women, regardless of age, offense, background, health, or maternal status, lived in the one limited space amid constant turmoil. Some prison officials even feared that the overcrowding, sickness, deaths of newborn babies, fights, screams, and attacks on guards might affect the safety, security, and health of male inmates. Chaplain B. C. Smith of Auburn Penitentiary in New York said in 1832 that to be a woman in prison was "worse than death."[6] On January 12, 1826, for example, Rachel Welsh died at Auburn during childbirth. She had become pregnant while incarcerated and then had been severely flogged. The attending doctor attributed her death to the beating. An outcry by reformers failed to stop floggings for other women prisoners; judges ruled they were necessary to keep order in prisons because inmates were not ordinary people and required physical force to make them obey. The public likewise believed women criminals were more depraved than men and beyond redemption. Only a few people, motivated by religious impulses, attempted to help them.[7]

WOMEN'S CORRECTIONS: THEORY AND PRACTICE

Elizabeth Gurney Fry, an English Quaker, established the theoretical and practical bases for women's corrections. In 1813 she volunteered to go to the women's section of Newgate Prison in London to teach and provide for the needs of children incarcerated with their mothers. She believed, as did most people, that the women were not redeemable and had not planned to help them. But she was horrified at the conditions in which the women lived, their treatment, and the hopelessness of their lives. Although it was considered extremely dangerous, Fry went into the prison to improve conditions for the women as well as for the children.[8]

She organized a volunteer group of women who conducted a school for the children, provided food, clothing, and work in prison for the inmates, and attempted to find jobs for them upon their release from Newgate. Their work demonstrated that even the most degraded women were redeemable. Fry's success in London brought about a significant change in attitudes toward the female convicts on the part of those interested in penal reform.[9]

With the change in attitude, Fry proposed a program that became basic to women's corrections. She said that female offenders had to be separated from male inmates and male guards. Therefore, separate women's correctional facilities were required, which were to be supervised and staffed only by women. Since order, discipline, and structure were necessary to reform the women, Fry recommended that women be classified and placed into specific treatment groups and programs for cleanliness, work, education, and religious instruction. Using volunteers and community resources, she provided humane treatment rather than physical punishment.[10]

Reformers in the United States moved to implement Fry's program. The first experiment took place in New York City in 1825 when John Griscom organized the Society for the Reformation of Juvenile Delinquents and established a House of Refuge. A separate building for female delinquents was opened under the combined superintendency of Sophia Wychoff, wife of a city alderman, and Sarah Hewhurst, sister of reform leader Isaac Collins. This was the first correctional experiment that used the theory that delinquent females, separated from males and taught by moral women, could be uplifted and reformed.[11]

Soon many private and religious societies were appearing in New York and other cities to help females. These societies established homes that were forerunners to modern halfway houses, where wayward and delinquent women could live, receive religious and vocational instruction, and medical care from Christian, moral women. Missionaries and volunteers were sent to the women's wards of almshouses, city jails and prisons, brothels and dancehalls to convince the women to reside in the homes and learn how to mend their ways. Women who went to the homes and were reformed were placed in jobs with good Christians so that they would not relapse into sin.[12]

In 1830, as a result of observing horrible conditions in New York City jails where women were kept, the Magdalen Society opened its home. In 1845 the Women's Prison Association (WPA) of New York City opened Hopper Home. (The association and the home are the oldest continuous establishments for assisting women offenders.) The two groups of women reformers provided nonlegal supervision for female offenders in the homes, applied the theories of Fry concerning separation, supervision of women, work, religion, education, discipline, and orderly lives, and helped reformed women find jobs, usually as domestics in Christian homes.[13]

The value of their work was recognized. The courts sent women thought to be redeemable to the homes in lieu of sending them to jail or prison, and assigned a matron to the Magdalen Home to assist in the supervision of the women and to report to the prison authorities. The work of these homes reinforced the concept that fallen women could be saved under the right circumstances, under the guidance of proper women.[14]

Except for these societies and homes in which women supervised women, incarcerated women continued to be supervised by men guards. This served to increase the demands of women reformers to place women professionals in corrections, for the experiences of the reformers proved that Fry's program could work in the United States. The next step was to move the program into the prisons and jails on a permanent basis.

From 1825 to 1873, reformers achieved a few successes in acquiring matrons for women. One of them involved Elizabeth Farnham, head matron of the women's section of Sing Sing from 1844 to 1848. Farnham was a feminist, reformer, wife of a lawyer, and friend of members of the Brook Farm intellectual circle in Massachusetts. She adopted Fry's program and added a component that made the program a model upon which U.S. women's corrections developed; she tried to make the prison environment like a home and have staff and inmates behave like a family.

Farnham believed that environmental conditions caused criminal behavior; therefore, changing the environment would change behavior. She proceeded to break the rules in the prison by ending the silent system, by grouping the women together for purposes of educational instruction rather than religious instruction, and by establishing a library of secular rather than religious books. She and her staff taught the women to read and write and instructed them in U.S. history, astronomy, geography, physiology, and personal hygiene. Literate women read books to those who could not read, even while the women worked. Farnham encouraged the women to become involved with handicrafts and all worked. She decorated the women's wing with pictures, maps, flowers, and lamps, and even brought in a piano for entertainment and holiday celebrations. Women from outside were invited to speak to the inmates, including Margaret Fuller, a writer and member of the Brook Farm circle. Alongside these innovative programs and services was a firm willingness to employ discipline if it was needed, for Farnham regarded self-control as necessary for true reformation. Solitary confinement was used when inmates did not respond to more gentle means.[15]

One of the most illuminating documents to come out of Farnham's group is a book by Georgiana Bruce Kirby, a matron and one of the Brook Farm circle, who wrote about the years she spent with Farnham at Sing Sing. Her book is important not only because it is one of the few sources from women who went on to beome the first corrections professionals, but also because it provides insights to the theories, problems, and public understanding of women in corrections. Kirby observed that educated women worked much better with inmates than did uneducated women because they had the discipline and ability to control the inmates. She nevertheless encountered criticism from some of her friends who held corrections work in low esteem: "It was natural that some of my old friends should be shocked on hearing that I had thus allied myself to the civilization we condemned."[16]

The Farnham approach, as described by Kirby, was the maternal one used by all professionals in that period:

> As I said, it had pleased us to love these low-down children of circumstances less fortunate than our own. We gloried in being able to lift a few of them out of the slough into which they had fallen, or in which they had been born, and to sustain them while they were trying to take a little step upward in the direction of the light.[17]

Despite successes, Farnham's approach, which seemed radical to many people, met criticism. After a power struggle with the conservatives, led by the institution's Protestant chaplain who did not approve of her secular program, she was dismissed in 1848. When Farnham departed for Boston to work with the handicapped, all her improvements at Sing Sing were eliminated and the women returned to neglect and ignorance.[18]

Setbacks such as dismissal of Farnham did not stop the efforts of the reformers, and their view of how women offenders should be treated gradually spread among professionals in the criminal justice system. The next step was to convince a male legislature to set up a separate women's prison and to hire women superintendents and matrons on a full-time and permanent basis. However, although men accepted the theory, they were not convinced that these pious, apparently passive, women could control female inmates.

The women answered that the force of their pure and upright characters would suffice; by establishing a domestic atmosphere in which virtues of motherhood and homemaking were stressed, feminine qualities would be elicited from the inmates. The legislators were impressed by both this argument and by reports prepared by the reformers of scandalous conditions in prisons where female inmates were guarded by men. Laws were passed creating institutions for women's corrections, with women in charge. The first one was the Indiana Reformatory Institution for Women and Girls, which opened in 1873 with Sarah Smith as superintendent. It was followed by reformatories in Framingham, Massachusetts, (1877); Bedford Hills, New York, (1901); and Clinton, New Jersey, (1913). In 1927, the Federal Reformatory at Alderson, West Virginia opened.[19]

The institutions had a common denominator: all were acquired as a result of efforts made by women's groups. Their members investigated the treatment of women in prison under male supervision, wrote reports, and lobbied the state and federal legislatures. Planners of the reformatories held to the basic theory of the unique capability of women to reform women offenders, and adopted Fry's program with the addition of the homelike atmosphere introduced by Farnham. The professional corrections women reinforced traditional women's roles and insured careers for themselves in corrections. Men in the profession permitted the women to be professionals because they knew and remained in their "place." By establishing a matriarchy in corrections, women did not compete with men.

THE SUPERINTENDENTS

The women who led these prisons were experienced in various aspects of social work and reform. Detailed information is available on seven of the first group of superintendents from 1884 to 1932: they were well-educated, three had a Ph.D. and one a B.A.; two were married; all were white; all had experience as nurses, teachers, matrons, or social workers; four actively supported women's rights; and all were experimenters and innovators. Jessie Hodder, for example, began a case study program and a work release program; Dr. Miriam Van Waters organized the Friendly Visitors, a community service volunteer group that is still in existence.[20]

Dr. Katherine B. Davis, as superintendent at Bedford Hills, New York, developed the case-study concept and also established a venereal disease clinic. In 1911, with funds from John D. Rockefeller, she opened the first center for the study of causes of female criminality. She became the first woman Commissioner of Corrections in New York City from 1914 to 1918, during which time she appointed her friend, Dr. Mary Harris, as superintendent of the women's division of the workhouse. Davis introduced reforms for all inmates in the city, and with Harris she made a number of changes that benefited women in particular, such as replacing striped uniforms with gingham dresses, getting shoes that fit, and engaging doctors to treat venereal diseases. Harris had the courtyard fenced in so for the first time in the history of the workhouse, women inmates could go outdoors while incarcerated.[21]

All the superintendents encouraged inmates to work and exercise outdoors as means of developing good work habits, relieving boredom and tension, and reducing the level of homosexual activity. In addition to educational and work programs, the concept of self-government was introduced in order to promote a sense of responsibility and citizenship among the inmates. The superintendents did the best they could with the small budgets given to operate women's prisons. As a result, treatment programs for drug addicts and alcoholics often were nonexistent. Harris lamented the lack of such programs and the resultant high rate of recidivism: "Unless we have built within them a wall of self-respect, moral integrity, and a desire to be an asset to the community instead of a menace, we have not protected society—which is ourselves—from the criminal."[22]

The first group of superintendents had to cope with problems that continue to the present: the lack of proper funding for rehabilitation programs and salaries, and the difficulty in attracting mature, educated, concerned women to work in the institutions. In 1934, a doctor, discussing her observations at a women's facility, wrote that a superintendent would have a hard time attracting and hiring capable officers, because she could offer a salary of only $45 per month with room and board, and the officer had to live in the prison 24 hours a day, with two days off every two weeks and two weeks vacation a year. She concluded: "This is not tempting bait to a woman of ability and when one also considers the fear, which any normal woman may be expected to have, of entering 'prison employment,' because of the physical risks she thinks she may run, it is a marvel that women's prisons recruit such able matrons and staff members. The movies and *Anne Vickers* do not help in popularizing this line of work as a career."[23]

Many of the programs created by women such as Harris and Davis were inspired by the social programs of settlement houses. The settlement house, a nineteenth century contribution to the need for social services in the rapidly growing industrialized cities of the East and Midwest, provided a homelike setting for workers, usually white, middle-class women who went out into the local community to perform their missions. Davis, like many women who eventually became active in corrections during the late nineteenth and early twentieth centuries, had once served in a settlement house.[24] The concept of a home, in which women lived and served others, was easily transferred to prisons when the women became superintendents. For many of the first professionals the institution became their homes, and the staff and inmates their families.

Ruth Collins, typical of this group of reformers, became the first superintendent of the House of Detention for Women (HDW) in New York City. She graduated from the University of Wisconsin and became an associate of Jane Addams at Hull House in Chicago. She also served as a juvenile worker in several cities, as head of the Women's Division of the House of Correction in Detroit, and as an administrator of the Social Service Division in the Bureau of Prisons of the Department of Justice in Washington, D.C. She operated the HDW with a social work approach, believing that women offenders needed education, cultural benefits, and time to think about how to change their lives.[25] In an interview in the *New*

York World Telegram in 1932, when she became superintendent of the House of Detention for Women, she said, "If we cannot send them out generally prepared for a new and better start, it is our fault and we have failed them. A prison is a place for restoration rather than for punishment."[26]

At the time when women such as Harris, Collins, and Davis were entering corrections as superintendents of prisons, it was extremely difficult for women with college degrees to obtain managerial positions in the private sector. Even at women's colleges they had a hard time becoming faculty or administrators, so great was the general prejudice against placing women in positions of responsibility. Ironically, the one area where they had a right to leadership was in women's corrections, where law, civil service specifications, or custom usually excluded men. It was common for women to remain in the corrections system for long periods of time because there were few outside opportunities. This may explain why so many educated and able women were willing to subject themselves to the many unpleasant aspects of life as a women's prison superintendent: they earned less than men superintendents; they were not expected to marry and have families, and the rural communities where most women's prisons were located expected a high degree of sexual morality and kept prominent women under the microscope of constant gossip; and, because of the rural environment, social opportunities were extremely limited.[27]

Only fairly recently has this changed, as women began to enter areas of the economy once reserved for men, and as the civil rights movement of the past 20 years threw down legal barriers and restrictions on employment. Now corrections professionals work as consultants or administrators in corrections departments and may even move into academia as faculty. For example, Laural Rans, former superintendent of the Iowa Women's Reformatory from 1967 to 1972, became a consultant. In June 1979 she received an appointment as Deputy Commissioner of the Illinois State Department of Correction. Katherine Gabel, a Ph.D. in sociology and an attorney, moved from superintendent of the Arizona Girls' School to Smith College as Dean of the School of Social Work and a lecturer in the Department of Sociology and Anthropology.[28]

Because of their education, participation in reform, and innovative contributions to corrections, these superintendents have gained the respect of both men and women in penal reform and corrections. Some of them are taking reform one step further and actively supporting women's equal employment rights in corrections and in the community.

THE CORRECTION OFFICERS

Although superintendents are the most visible women in corrections, they are far outnumbered by the women correction officers, or, as they were usually called before the 1960s, matrons. For the nineteenth and early twentieth century, most information about them comes from reports, articles, and autobiographies of superintendents and a few former inmates. Kate O'Hare, imprisoned in 1919 for a federal offense under the Espionage Act, wrote of her experiences at the state prison in Jefferson City, Missouri. It was a men's prison with a special section for women; a male warden was in charge of a chief matron and subordinate matrons. O'Hare criticized the matrons, although she sympathized with many of the problems they faced:

> The matrons were required to live in the prison and were never, except on rare leaves of absence, out of the sights and sounds and smells of prison. They were prisoners to almost the same degree that we were, and they all staggered under a load of responsibility far too great for their limited intelligence and untrained powers. They handled human beings at their worst, and under the worst possible conditions, and saw nothing day or night but sordid, ugly things ungilded by the glow of hope or love.[29]

She described the sadness of the lives of these women:

> These women who were our keepers had missed love and wifehood; they had nothing to look back upon or forward to. There is a sort of stigma attached to their work that makes the possibilities of love and mating for them very limited indeed. The ordinary social relations of normal life were impossible for them, and they lived in a very inferno of loneliness and isolation![30]

O'Hare's description of the problems of matrons, both on the job and in their personal lives, is one of the best available. She was able to understand and explain to readers what it was to be a matron. She was explicit in her descriptions of their corruption and harsh treatment of the inmates, much of which, she thought, resulted from the stigma attached to corrections that destroyed inmates and matrons.[31]

Many of these problems still exist. The job of prison guard is still not considered proper women's work by the public, and within the corrections profession the status of women professionals is so low that they have been ignored in almost all books on corrections and studies of correction officers. No studies were made of women officers until 1979, when state studies were undertaken in California and South Carolina and a national study was initiated by the Center for Women's Policy Studies in Washington, D.C.

Training is still often inadequate. Until the federal prison system instituted formal training at an academy in 1971, training for women officers normally took place in the women's prison at Alderson. New York City opened its academy and started formal training in 1957; New Jersey has a training academy but it is not mandatory, and sometimes officers are assigned to it after they have been on the job for years. Although most states offer some type of training, most counties and cities do not; the officer is given a key and told to go to work.[32]

Correction officers still must face the problem of dealing with an extremely diverse group of women inmates, sentenced for a wide variety of crimes, and often under serious emotional stress. Since most states have only one women's facility, if any, and women's jails exist in only ten cities in the entire country, women usually are incarcerated in the one institution. This includes all women over 16, with every type of criminal history and security classification, diverse levels of education and skills, emotional maturity, family experiences, and problems. Reports from state and federal facilities in the 1970s indicate an increase in the number of emotionally disturbed women coming into the facilities, perhaps related to drug abuse. Many of the inmates are in emotional turmoil. It is not uncommon for a pregnant woman to be incarcerated and to have her child while still under custody. Officers therefore must cope with the special needs of a pregnant woman, the stress of having a child while incarcerated, and the separation trauma that occurs after the baby has been taken away, not to be seen perhaps until the mother is released. Women who have families worry about their children, some of whom are placed in foster care. Because most incarcerated women are mothers, but few are married, they must bear the burden of caring for the children. The geographic location of the institution often makes it difficult, if not impossible, for the women to have visits from their children.[33]

Geography also plays a role in another problem, that of attracting and keeping a qualified staff. Because women's prisons are located in rural or suburban areas, it becomes difficult to recruit staff, except from the local communities. Women from cities are reluctant to travel long distances to the prison or to move to these isolated communities. The warden of the women's prison in New Jersey commented that he was "scraping the bottom of the barrel" of the civil service list.[34] Turnover in staff is high because women move to cities for other jobs as soon as possible. Recruiting from local communities often produces sharp differences in the race, religion, and life-styles of inmates and staff.

Women's jails are easier to staff because they are located in cities. In addition, since the 1950s it has been more likely that the staff in the jails will be similar to the racial and religious backgrounds of the inmates. In New York City, the staff in 1976 was over 90 percent black and the inmates 85 percent black; many of the staff shared similar socioeconomic backgrounds with the inmates, often living in the same neighborhoods.[35]

Geographic location also can affect staff morale. For example, when the women's jail in New York City was moved from Greenwich Village, in the heart of Manhattan, to Rikers Island in Queens, morale dropped and several officers retired or resigned. In Greenwich Village the officers were within walking distance of public transportation, banks, and stores. It was easy for them to get to and from work and to take care of their personal and family needs either before starting work or after finishing their tour of duty. These services were not conveniently located near Rikers Island; it became necessary for most of the women to have cars for transportation. Absenteeism rose as women took time off to care for their personal and family needs.[36]

Correction officers also must cope with the fact that they work in what is called the "locked-in culture." Like women in some other kinds of employment, correction officers often must work holidays or night shifts. However, when they do so, they are literally locked in the institution for the entire period of their duty. They may not leave the institution for any reason, and in that sense are as incarcerated as the inmates. After their eight-hour shift, they may be obliged to work an additional eight-hour shift if an officer on the next shift fails to report for duty. If the officers remain after the first few years, they tend to stay until retirement. Some officers become "job phobic" from the emotional stress and the locked-in culture.[37]

The isolation and harsh working conditions of prison life are therefore factors working against the entrance of women into corrections, but obviously women enter anyway. The major attraction seems to be money. In rural areas even low salaries are better than nothing. According to Elizabeth G. Flynn, incarcerated at the Alderson federal prison from 1955 to 1957 for violating the Smith Act, most of the matrons were white rural people from the immediate vicinity. They worked for the money, not from any sense of dedication; the turnover rate was high because many left for better jobs in cities and others quit when they married.[38]

This is a familiar pattern in many states, but it is not easy to generalize because conditions vary so much across the country. It is not unusual to find starting salaries as low as $6,000, but most are higher. In 1979 the Federal Bureau of Prisons started their correction officers at $11,712; New Jersey started at $11,364, with the possibility of earning up to $20,000 a year, including overtime and differential pay for night work. In the spring of 1979 the New York City Department of Correction advertised for the position of correction officer. Men, women, and minority group members were encouraged to file for the civil service examination. They were told that the starting salary was $15,247 with raises to $19,341 in three years, plus benefits and 20 paid vacation days from the first year. To qualify, a person need only be a citizen and have a high school diploma or equivalent.[39]

This should be compared with conditions in 1951, when in New York City a woman correction officer started at $3,000 per year. By 1971 the starting salary had risen to $10,000. Simultaneously, there was a change in educational requirements. In 1951 the officer needed no formal education, but by 1971 the job required a high school diploma or a general education diploma (GED). However, New York City is not typical of all corrections departments. In over half of all correctional jurisdictions, especially on the county and city levels, no high school diploma is required. In these areas in 1979 the salary could be as low as $6,000 per year.[40]

Another change has taken place since 1950. College-educated women have turned their backs on corrections, preferring probation, parole, and law enforcement careers. During the Depression of the 1920s and 1930s, college-educated women took as many civil service examinations as possible and many were appointed from the correction officer list. It may not have been their first choice, but it provided them with steady work and an income. Because of their education, they rose quickly through civil service examinations to become superintendents, as was the case of three women who became officers in the House of Detention for Women in New York City in the late 1930s and early 1940s, a period of time when an estimated 25 percent of the officers had college degrees. Now, however, with other job opportunities available, college-educated women will not be attracted to corrections for careers as officers.[41]

DISCRIMINATION

The final major problems associated with women in corrections are the various forms of discrimination. Major changes have occurred during the past two decades that have opened new areas to women. Nevertheless, progress is uneven, and while the courts extend women's opportunities in one area, they may restrict them in others.

The most recent form of discrimination is the veterans' preference laws, which benefit mostly men. Women who score higher than veterans on civil service examinations receive lower places than men on appointment and promotion lists and get less consideration for assignments. In June 1979 the U.S. Supreme Court upheld by seven to two the Massachusetts veterans' preference law, on the basis that the law was not gender-based because it put both men and women at a disadvantage as individuals, even though it did benefit men as a class.[42]

A much older form of discrimination is racial. Before the Brown decision in 1954, all superintendents were white, although there were black officers. It was not unusual for black officers, even those with college degrees, to be assigned the most menial and physically strenuous work available in the institution. For example, Flynn, writing of her experiences as an inmate at Alderson in the 1950s, explained how the black officers and black inmates were always assigned to the piggery. In the House of Detention for Women in New York City, black officers and inmates were assigned to housing areas called "black corridors." The black inmates worked in the laundry, while white inmates worked in the kitchen. Three former superintendents of the HDW (from 1967 to 1978) agreed that once segregation ceased to be official policy, racial discrimination ceased to be practiced. The change occurred because more black women became officers, and in 1969 the first black woman became superintendent.[43]

Since the 1950s, noticeable changes have occurred in correctional staffs. The number of black officers and administrators has increased, especially in urban areas. Black women found that civil service employment offered them steady, full-time work, a good income and fringe benefits, and the opportunity for promotion based on competitive examinations where racial discrimination would not interfere with advancement. This trend is particularly noticeable in the women's jails in large cities such as New York, Los Angeles, and Chicago.[44]

The third form of discrimination involving women is sexual. Whatever their race, religion, or ethnic stock, all women have encountered discrimination, some subtle, most quite blatant, in the corrections system. For example, men always have been permitted to be wardens of women's institutions but, until the 1970s, women have been excluded from men's institutions. Men were assigned to women's facilities in security, maintenance, and administrative work, but women were not assigned to men's facilities until the late 1960s. Not until the 1970s were women officers assigned to duties other than searching women visitors. Rarely did a woman work in the central offices of a department of corrections, even if the commissioner was a woman, as happened twice in New York City (Katherine B. Davis, 1914–18 and Anna M. Kross, 1954–65). Women superintendents and officers have received lower salaries and less money for programs than men. Because women inmates seldom riot, escape, or commit violent acts on themselves or others, they are not considered security risks and accordingly less need is felt to supply additional corrections personnel. A woman superintendent in a meeting with the commissioner and male warden is often a single voice and vote for issues concerning women.[45]

The roots of sexual discrimination go far back into history, and the embodiment of discrimination in law and policy has characterized U.S. life. But in practical terms, discrimination is confronted by women most often in the personal views and biases of the men who compose most of the personnel in corrections. The author has had considerable exposure to the views of both men and women officers, especially in a course entitled "Women's Corrections" that she teaches at the New Jersey Department of Corrections Training Academy. Since she is not responsible for assigning any grades, the class discussions are open and unrestrained, sometimes emotionally charged. These classes have corroborated impressions gained while visiting jails and prisons. Men continue to see women in traditional ways: the good woman is the mother who stays at home; a working woman is suspect; and a woman who works in a jail or prison, particularly a male facility, is suspect, considered "loose" at best.

Since the 1970s, local and state departments of corrections have been forced to comply with federal legislation forbidding employment discrimination based on sex. Title VII of the Civil Rights Act of 1964, which forbade discrimination on the basis of sex, gave women a legal basis on which to speak out against unfair practices and conditions in the corrections system. The act's real effects, however, were limited because it did not include employees of state, county, or city governments. Only in 1972 was it amended, broadening the powers of the Equal Employment Opportunity Commission (EEOC), to cover all government agencies. Discriminatory practices were forbidden to all agencies receiving Law Enforcement Assistance Administration funds. This was restated in the 1973 and 1976 amendments to the 1968 Crime Control Act: no private, state, local, or federal agency may receive LEAA funds if discrimination by sex is found. Since departments of corrections all over the country rely heavily on LEAA funds, they have made efforts to comply with the new laws.

As a result, women correction officers have been assigned to male institutions and men to women's in direct contact with inmates of the opposite sex. Gloria Lee was appointed warden at the Men's House of Detention, Bronx, New York; Janice Warne at the Albion Correctional Institution, New York; Arleene Love at the Deberry Correctional Institute for Special Needs Offenders, Nashville, Tennessee; Norma Gluckstern at the facility for emotionally ill inmates at Heightfield, Maryland; and Margaret Hambreck at the Federal Correctional Institution, Morgantown, West Virginia. At the same time, male wardens were appointed to three women's facilities for the first time in their history: the federal prison at Alderson, West Virginia, the state prison at Clinton, New Jersey, and the city jail in New York City.[46]

By 1979, 33 states and many cities had complied, assigning women to male institutions, but only California and Delaware had integrated men and women officers and assigned them on an equal basis. The Department of Corrections of California has been especially forthcoming in its efforts. Prior to 1972, no women worked in male institutions. From 1972 to 1974, women officers were assigned to men's institutions only to search and supervise women visitors to prevent the smuggling of contraband. As a result of pressure exerted on the Director of Corrections, Raymond Procunier, by the chief of personnel and by the only woman executive in the department, the policy for full integration of staff went into effect in mid-1974. Women who apply for positions in male institutions in nontraditional job assignments receive the training and supervision necessary for the job. As Arlene M. Becker, Deputy Director of the department wrote: "The department cannot supervise the feelings and opinions of the managers, but it can supervise their behavior."[47] The male managers of male institutions are assured that the women assigned to their facilities will do the same work and meet the same standards as the men. This policy and Procunier's support have been crucial to the success of equal employment opportunity in California's corrections system.[48]

New York City began to end sex discrimination in 1978 when a new commissioner of correction, a woman deputy, and a woman assistant commissioner began to change policies. The next year the city personnel director deleted the word superintendent, which had applied only to women in charge of the women's jail, from job designations and substituted the title of warden for both sexes. Sex designation for all other titles was eliminated. After the changes were made, Gloria Lee became warden of the House of Detention for Men in the Bronx and Albert Nolen became acting warden of the New York City Correctional Institution For Women on Rikers Island. For the first time, two women officers have been assigned to key positions at central headquarters, one to the Communications Control Center and one to the Chief of Operations Office. However, for reasons of security and privacy, women officers are assigned primarily to the women's jail.[49]

The federal prison system also has attempted to break discriminatory practices. Sylvia G. McCollum of the Federal Bureau of Prisons (FBP) wrote: "The federal government is the largest single employer in the United States. What it does—and equally important, what it fails to do—in employment practices is critical."[50] As late as 1975 the FBP began implementing an affirmative action program that included the Women's Program, which was to advise the Equal Employment Opportunities Commission on issues concerning women in corrections, and the Upward Mobility Program, which would insure that women have an opportunity for advancement in the system. The Bureau of Prisons has acted to promote women to supervisory and training positions, as well as to integrate men and women officers into a single correctional staff in all but the maximum security penitentiaries.[51]

According to Richard Lyle, chief of the Equal Employment Opportunity Section of the Bureau of Prisons, there were 345 women officers as of March 31, 1979, comprising 16.5 percent of the total correction officer staff. The starting salary is $11,712, increasing after one year to $13,014; the maximum salary for an officer is $16,920. A warden earns from $38,160 to $47,500. As of 1979, only one woman, Margaret Hambreck, was a warden of a male facility. She worked at the Federal Correctional Institution at Morgantown, West Virginia, a minimum security facility for young men. Women were associate wardens at the women's facilities at Alderson, West Virginia, and at Pleasanton, California. Both of these women's institutions had male wardens for the first time in the history of federal women's corrections.[52]

In 1971 when the FBP started formal uniform training for officers and instituted one program for both sexes. Instructors at the three training academies are both men and women. In fact, the director at the Denver, Colorado Training Academy is a woman, Charlotte Byerly. Women are supposed to comprise 10 percent of the staff of male facilities (although they are not assigned to any posts in maximum security facilities); men are assigned to the women's institutions as well. For example, at Alderson in 1979 there were 70 women and 42 men correction officers.[53]

Sam Sample, in charge of training programs for the Bureau of Prisons, commented that women who stick it out in corrections are the most persevering people in the world. They have to overcome enormous and subtle obstacles placed in their way by men in the system. There are fewer problems, however, in cocorrectional facilities such as Fort Worth, Texas and Lexington, Kentucky, than there are in all male institutions. Sample also noted that the location of the facility affects acceptance of women in male institutions, with women in rural areas least likely to be accepted.[54]

Despite federal legislation, women continue to encounter hostility and resistance from male officers. One reason that is often given for not having women officers integrated with men in male facilities is the question of inmate privacy. In most prisons and jails, cells have bars, not doors. All the actions of the inmates are visible to other inmates and to the staff. If toilets are outside the cells, they are open and arranged so that the officers can supervise; the same is true of showers. Since 1970 there have been about a dozen lawsuits by inmates who claimed that their rights to privacy have been violated by women officers. The women filed countersuits, claiming that they were denied equal opportunity to assignments in male facilities because of the privacy issue. It is a classic case of the collision of two constitutionally protected rights.

In New Jersey, the state attorney general declared that just as members of the opposite sex do not work in public bathrooms, so in the state's correctional institutions members of the opposite sex should not work in the housing areas of inmates. In other cases, *Bonner v. Coughlin* in 1975, *Hodges v. Klein* in 1976, and *Frasier v. Ward* in 1977, the courts have supported inmates' rights to privacy, basing their decisions on the Fourth and Eighth Amendments. In *Re Long* in 1976 and *Forts v. Ward* in 1978, the courts relied on the Fourteenth Amendment to insure the protection of inmates' rights to privacy. *Forts v. Ward* was the only case brought by women inmates against male officers. The inmates at Bedford Hills, New York, charged in a class-action suit that the prison's 43 men officers violated the privacy of the 407 women inmates. However, the courts have not ignored equal employment issues. In the *Long* and *Forts* cases, as well as in *Reynolds v. Wise* in 1974 and *Meith v. Dothard* in 1976, the courts stated that women and men officers should be given selective work assignments so as not to interfere with the rights of inmates.[55]

Women officers were excluded from working in male institutions in *Dothard v. Rawlinson* in 1977, the *City of Philadelphia v. Pennsylvania Human Relations Commission* in 1973, and the *Iowa Department of Social Services v. Iowa Merit Employment Department* in 1977. These decisions were based on the bona fide occupational qualifications (BFOQ) exception to the Title VII ban on sex discrimination in employment. The courts decided that in male maximum security institutions where women officers are in physical danger, and in institutions where the rights to privacy of males are at issue, women come under the BFOQ exception and can be denied employment. The danger exists that corrections departments might use the BFOQ as justification to prevent the integration of male and female officers into one correctional staff with equal employment rights.[56]

The restrictions placed by the courts forbidding women officers to move freely in men's facilities have raised the issue of whether women so restricted can be effective members of the corrections staff. Marvin Frankel, federal judge in the New York State district, issued a "knock first" rule for the Federal Metropolitan Correctional Center in New York City. An officer must knock on doors to alert inmates that he or she is entering the housing area or toilet/shower area. However, this also alerts inmates to the fact that an officer is coming and can interfere with security. This obviously is a convenient argument for persons who seek to prevent women from expanding their role in corrections.[57]

Yet men have been supervisors, administrators, and wardens in women's institutions throughout the past century. Men wardens are in charge of the federal prisons for women at Alderson and Pleasanton, the women's prison in Jessup, Maryland, and the women's jail in New York City, to name but a few. It might be asked how they can attend to the safety and security of these institutions if they are not free to enter all areas. The question is thus not one of women in men's prisons only, and no resolution will come until there is some discussion of the role of men in women's prisons.

One of the most promising attempts to solve this problem has been made in the California state prison system. According to assistant director Arlene M. Becker, the problems of searching inmates and supervising toilet and bathing facilities have been successfully met. Women officers do not, as a general rule, do skin searches of male inmates, nor do men officers search female inmates. Screening has been put up in the shower and toilet facilities so that only the upper portion of the body is exposed; windows have been fogged. Inmates who follow the rules retain their privacy.[58]

Since this policy went into effect, inmates have had no complaints and officers have encountered no insoluble difficulties. Becker thinks that male inmates actually have been better behaved, less profane, and more concerned with their hygiene and appearance than before the women appeared. Male officers also are showing more respect for the privacy of inmates.[59]

PERFORMANCE STUDIES

The generally favorable results in California have been repeated also in Colorado. From July 1976 to June 1977 the men's jail in Boulder was the subject of the most comprehensive study yet done of the effects of women officers in male institutions. The researchers questioned inmates and officers, both male and female, on issues of rights to privacy, resentment among inmates and male officers, sexual frustration for inmates, and security and discipline in the jail. Ten women were hired to work in the county jail for men and to perform all the duties of men officers except strip searches.[60]

The Boulder study reported that inmates, male officers, and female officers were satisfied with the results, that is, the experiment was a success. Specifically, the majority of inmates felt no invasion of privacy, no resentment at having to take orders from women, no sexual frustration, could not manipulate the women any more than they could the men, and did not feel any more protective of the women whom they cursed as they did the men, until they realized that the verbal abuse had no apparent effect on the women's effectiveness as officers. Male officers did not resent working with women and believed that the presence of women reduced tensions, brought a softening effect that reduced violence, and had the effect of "increasing the livability of the institution."[61]

Male and female officers thought women could be just as effective as men in the same jobs except in stopping fights, where the women were at a physical disadvantage. Even the matter of physical strength, which might seem beyond question, is not so simple. Affirmative action policies have reduced height and weight requirements to enable Hispanic and Oriental men to qualify for corrections work; some male officers are smaller than some of the women. The issue therefore is not size so much as training in self-defense and in handling fights. Such programs as exist have major flaws, relating mostly to men's attitudes toward women. In the federal and state systems, where since the 1970s men and women have been trained together, women are sometimes treated too harshly or too leniently by the instructors, who are usually men. Some instructors even pair women in the one-on-one sessions, with the result that the women get no experience in handling even simulated fights with men. If these inequalities in training could be reduced, women officers would be much better able to cope with conditions in men's facilities.[62]

DIVISION OVER GOALS

The issue of training is one area of disagreement among women correction officers. The women who seek equality of opportunity in the profession (the integrationists) want to be fully trained and prepared to accept any assignment in both men's and women's institutions. However, not all the women want equality of opportunity with men. The traditionalists prefer to work in a women's facility. They have no desire to participate in the physical training programs conducted at corrections academies. Furthermore, when working with men officers in a women's or a men's prison or jail, they assume the traditional women's role and expect men to do the heavy work. They provide a convenient example for any man who claims that in reality most women do not want to change the old ways.[63]

The burden on the women who want change is thus very great; they must deal with the contrary views of both men and women. Invariably they must be a cut above the norm, must work harder to prove themselves to the men officers and administrators, and often must get the job done without the help and advice of colleagues. And all the while they must act pleasantly and not show resentment or insubordination. To do this, usually with the support of only a few women coworkers, creates pressures; "messes their heads" is the phrase used. The task is made more difficult by the low esteem in which the women are held by most men officers and administrators, and by the open opposition of these men to working with women. The integrationists face not only the open hostility, but also sexual innuendo and harassment.[64]

Women who do speak out face the risk of being punished, if only informally, in a variety of ways: by being transferred to another institution, by a lack of cooperation from male colleagues, or by constant reminders that they are not trusted because they are incapable of doing the same jobs as men. The outspoken deputy warden in charge of the training academy in New York City was transferred twice in one year. Another woman, actively seeking equality for women in the profession, faced many obstacles in order to gain a position at central headquarters as an administrator. In an attempt to scare her away from the position, she was sent to supervise correction officers training at the firing range where live ammunition was used, without the benefit of advice or instructions.[65]

THE FUTURE

Perhaps these factors are responsible for the small growth in the proportion of women in corrections over the past decade. In 1973 there were 5,227 women officers and 51,546 men officers; women were only 9.2 percent of all officers. In 1977, there were 8,169 women and 62,743 men officers; women were 11.5 percent of all officers. The federal system has not yet reached its quota of 10 percent women staff in its male prisons. In California there were 300 women and 3,000 men officers in 1979.[66]

While much has been done to reduce the level of sexual discrimination, a great deal remains. Aside from the strong biases that exist in the minds and emotions of men, there are specific inequities that persist. Except in California, Delaware, and the federal prison system, women officers continue to be concentrated in women's facilities. The small number of women in corrections, 11.5 percent of the officers and 1 percent of the administrators nationwide, means that most of them are needed in women's institutions in order to comply with the inmates' rights to privacy as mandated by the courts.

Although it has been demonstrated that women officers are as effective and competent as men, women will continue to be kept from advancing within corrections. Veterans' preference laws will keep women from being promoted and assigned to desirable posts, and even in an integrated system these laws will reduce the possibility of women becoming supervisors and administrators. Perhaps the greatest obstacles are inmates' rights to privacy and the bona fide occupational qualification exemptions to Title VII that the courts have upheld in suits seeking to prevent women from working in male facilities.

Corrections is supported by tax money. The tax revolt mentality of California's Proposition 13 is spreading and other states and cities have cut their budgets. Corrections, the lowest on the priority list in the criminal justice system, and recipient of the smallest slice of the system's budget, will feel the impact and fewer people will be hired. The few women hired will be assigned to women's prisons and jails.

Finally, women in corrections lack an organization, formal or informal, that can lobby for them. Women are excluded from the "old boys" network that binds male correction officers together. As in any profession, this network is the best way to familiarize oneself with the inner workings of the system and to make contacts that will help in securing assignments and promotions. Although the network is not tangible or formal in any given facility or system, its existence is essential to the officers in many ways.

One answer for women is to form an "old girls" network, as is generally happening in many professions, such as law enforcement and the law. But women correction officers have unique disadvantages in this regard. The number of women's institutions is small and the facilities are widely dispersed across the country. There has not developed any tradition of becoming vocal and active on corrections issues; support groups have not emerged even in large cities where there may be many women in corrections.

Unlike women in law enforcement and the legal profession, those in corrections are not active and articulate on issues concerning their careers, nor do they have national or local organizations. Lacking support both within corrections and in the community, women in corrections who want equality often have to make that effort on an individual basis. The odds are against them.

NOTES

1. Carroll Smith-Rosenberg, "Beauty, the Beast and the Militant Woman: A Case Study in Sex Roles and Social Stress in Jacksonian America,' in *Many Pasts: Readings in*

American Social History, 1600–1876, ed. Herbert G. Gutman and Gregory S. Kealey (Englewood Cliffs, N.J.: Prentice-Hall, 1973), pp. 287–305; Eleanor Flexner, *Century of Struggle: The Woman's Rights Movement in the United States* (New York: Atheneum, 1971), pp. 23–70, and 179–215; David J. Pivar, *Purity Crusade: Sexual Morality and Social Control, 1868–1900* (Westport, Conn.: Greenwood Press, 1973), pp. 50–73; Alice Felt Tyler, *Freedom's Ferment: Phases of American Social History from the Colonial Period to the Outbreak of the Civil War* (New York: Harper Torchbooks, 1962), pp. 227–462; Allen F. Davis, *Spearheads for Reform: The Social Settlements and the Progressive Movement 1890–1914* (New York: Oxford University Press, 1967), passim; and Barbara Welter, "The Cult of True Womanhood: 1820–1860," in *Our American Sisters: Women in American Life and Thought,* ed. Jean E. Friedman and William G. Shade (Boston: Allyn and Bacon, 1973), pp. 96–123.

2. Smith-Rosenberg, op. cit., pp. 200–2; and 288–96; Pivar, op. cit., pp. 18–43; Estelle B. Freedman, "Their Sisters' Keepers: An Historical Perspective on Female Correctional Institutions in the United States: 1870–1900," *Feminist Studies* 2 (1974): 82–83.

3. Smith-Rosenberg, op. cit., pp. 288–95; and Pivar, op. cit., pp. 24–32.

4. Smith-Rosenberg, op. cit., pp. 300–1.

5. Richard Hofstadter, *The Age of Reform* (New York: Vintage Books, 1955), pp. 174–86; and Philip Klein, *Prison Methods in New York State: Studies in History, Economics and Public Law* (New York: Longmans, Green, 1920), p. 45.

6. David W. Lewis, *From Newgate to Dannemora: The Rise of the Penitentiary in New York, 1796–1848* (Ithaca, N.Y.: Cornell University Press, 1965), pp. 162–64.

7. Ibid., pp. 94–97, 155–59, 162–64, and 173–75; Klein, op. cit., pp. 41–45; Freedman, op. cit., pp. 77–79; and Clarice Feinman, "Imprisoned Women: A History of the Treatment of Women Incarcerated in New York City, 1932–1975" (Ph.D. diss., New York University, 1976), pp. 22–40.

8. Lewis, op. cit., p. 160; and Freedman, op. cit., pp. 79–80.

9. Ibid.

10. Ibid.

11. Klein, op. cit., pp. 225–26; Freedman, op. cit., p. 80; John F. Richmond, *New York and its Institutions, 1609–1872* (New York: E. B. Treat, 1872), pp. 317–20 and 457–60; and Lewis, op. cit., pp. 160–61.

12. Richmond, op. cit., pp. 317–476.

13. Ibid., pp. 317–20, and 457–60.

14. Klein, op. cit., p. 374.

15. Lewis, op. cit., pp. 237–41; and Georgiana B. Kirby, *Years of Experience: An Autobiographical Narrative* (1887; reprint ed., New York: AMS Press, 1971), pp. 190–211.

16. Kirby, op. cit., pp. 194 and 199–200.

17. Ibid., pp. 225–26.

18. Lewis, op. cit., pp. 242–50.

19. Freedman, op. cit., pp. 86–88.

20. *Notable American Women 1607–1950: A Biographical Dictionary* (Cambridge, Mass.: Belknap Press, 1971), vol. I, pp. 439–41; vol. II, pp. 197–99 and 277–78; Claudine Schweber, "Mary Belle Harris," A biographical essay in *Notable American Women* (Cambridge, Mass.: Harvard University Press, forthcoming); and Burton Rowles, *The Lady at Box 99: The Story of Miriam Van Waters* (Greenwich, Conn.: Seabury Press, 1962), pp. 31–33 and 260–70; and Feinman, op. cit., pp. 279–80.

21. Feinman, op. cit., pp. 49–53; Mary Harris, *I Knew Them in Prison* (New York: Viking Press, 1936), pp 28–34 and 43–49; Women's Prison Association, *Annual Report* 1915, pp. 34–35; *1917,* p. 30; and *1929,* p. 15

22. Harris, op. cit., pp. 43–49 and 382–401.

23. Ibid., pp. 88–91; Ellen C. Potter, "The Problem of Women in Penal and Correctional Institutions," *Quarterly Journal of Corrections* 1 (Fall 1977):13; and Florence Monahan, *Women in Crime* (New York: Ives Washburn, 1941), pp. 43–44.

24. Davis, op. cit., pp. 23 and 187.

25. Feinman, op. cit., p. 71; and Prison Association of New York, *Annual Report 1933*, p. 42.

26. Feinman, op. cit., pp. 71–72.

27. Potter, op. cit., pp. 13–14.

28. "Profile," *Quarterly Journal of Corrections* 1 (Fall 1977): 7–9.

29. Kate R. O'Hare, *In Prison* (1923; reprint ed., Seattle, Wash.: University of Washington Press, 1976), p. 162.

30. Ibid.

31. Ibid., pp. 161–63.

32. Interview, Marie D. Miller, county training supervisor, New Jersey Department of Corrections Training Academy, December 13, 1978; interview, Sam Samples, Staff Training Development, Federal Bureau of Prisons, June 22, 1979; New York City Department of Correction, *Annual Report 1950*, pp. 28 and 30; *1952*, pp. 3 and 25; *1953*, p. v; *1955*, pp. xv–xvi; *1957*, pp. 11–13; and *1958*, p. 78.

33. Judy Sammon, "Campus Look is Sharp Contrast to Reality of Penitentiary Walls," *Quarterly Journal of Corrections* 1 (Fall 1977): 47; interview, Sherry MacPhearson, Professional Services, Correctional Institution for Women, Clinton, N.J., May 3, 1979; interview, Essie O. Murph, superintendent, New York City Correctional Institution for Women, January 16, 1976; and Phyllis Jo Baunach, "Effects of the Mother-Child Separation on Inmate-Mothers" (Paper presented at the Annual Meeting of the American Society of Criminology, 1978), pp. 1–12.

34. Interview, Philip Dwyer, superintendent, Correctional Institution for Women, Clinton, N. J., May 1, 1979.

35. Interview, Murph, op. cit.; and Clarice Feinman, "An Afro-American Experience: The Women in New York City's Jail," *Afro-Americans in New York Life and History* 1 (July 1977): 202–3.

36. Interview, Murph, op. cit.; and Feinman, "Imprisoned Women," op. cit., pp. 163–65.

37. Interview, Miller, op. cit.; interview, Debora Cohn, director of labor relations, New York City Department of Corrections, May 4, 1979; interview, Jean Wolfe, research analyst, State of California Department of Corrections, July 9, 1979; and interview, MacPhearson, op. cit.

38. Elizabeth G. Flynn, *The Alderson Story: My Life as a Political Prisoner* (New York: International Publishers, 1972), pp. 94–95.

39. Interview, Cohn, op. cit.; interview, William T. McClammy, county training specialist, New Jersey Department of Corrections Training Academy, August 6, 1979; and interview, Richard Lyle, chief of Equal Employment Opportunity Section, Federal Bureau of Prisons, June 21, 1979.

40. Municipal Reference Library, New York City, "Civil Service Announcements Folder."

41. Letter from Mary K. Lindsay, former superintendent, House of Detention for Women, New York City, to Clarice Feinman, February 25, 1974; interview, Murph, op. cit.; interview, Florence Holland, former superintendent, House of Detention for Women, New York City, April 8, 1974; and interview, Jessie L. Behagen, former Superintendent, House of Detention for Women, New York City, April 20, 1974.

42. *New York Times*, June 10, 1979, p. 20E.

43. Flynn, op. cit., pp. 97–99; and interviews, Murph, Holland, Behagen, op. cit.

44. Interview, Murph, op. cit.; interview, Cynthia Anderson, sergeant, Sybil Brand Institute, Los Angeles, Calif., May 7, 1978.

45. Interview, Miller, op. cit.; interview, Cohn, op. cit.; interview, Samples, op. cit.; interview, Lyle, op. cit.; and interview, Arlene Becker, assistant director, State of California Department of Corrections, May 18, 1979.

46. Interview, Lyle, op.cit.; interview, Samples, op.cit.; interview, Cohn, op.cit.; interview, Dwyer, op.cit.; "Profile," op. cit., pp. 7–8; "Men and Women," *Crime and Delinquency* 22 (January 1976): 107; and "N.Y. Women Inmates Sue State Over Posting of Male Officers," *Corrections Digest* 8 (April 13, 1977): 10.

47. "CONtact Information" (Lincoln, Neb.: CONtact Center, 1979), reprint; and Arlene Becker, "Women in Corrections: A Process of Change," *Resolution* 1 (Summer 1975): 19–21.

48. Becker, op. cit.; and interview, Becker, op.cit.

49. Interview, Cohn, op. cit.

50. Sylvia G. McCollum, "The Federal Government and Affirmative Action: A Default of Leadership," *Resolution* 1 (Summer 1975): 11.

51. Interview, Lyle, op.cit.

52. Interview, Lyle, op.cit.; and interview, Samples, op.cit.

53. Ibid.

54. Interview, Samples, op. cit.

55. Interview, Miller, op. cit.; and Susan L. Reisner, "Balancing Inmates' Right to Privacy with Equal Employment for Prison Guards," *Women's Rights Reporter* 4 (Summer 1978): 243–50.

56. Reisner, op. cit.

57. Gillian Sacks, "Prisoner Privacy and Equal Employment Opportunities" (University of Connecticut School of Law: Special Research Project, 1979), p. 14.

58. Becker, op. cit. p. 21; and interview, Becker, op.cit.

59. Ibid.

60. Peter J. Kissel and Paul L. Katsampes, "The Impact of Women Corrections Officers on the Functioning of Institutions Housing Male Inmates," unpublished paper (Boulder, Colo.: National Institute of Corrections Jail Center, 1979), pp. 1–8.

61. Ibid., pp. 27–32.

62. Interview, Becker, op.cit.; interview, Miller, op.cit.; interview, Cohn, op.cit.; and interview, Samples, op.cit.

63. Interview, Miller, op.cit.; interview, Becker, op.cit.; interview, Wolfe, op.cit.; and interview, Cohn, op.cit.

64. Ibid.

65. Interview, Miller, op.cit.; and interview, Cohn, op.cit.

66. Interview, Betty Minor, assistant project director, Center for Women's Policy Studies, Washington, D.C.; interview, Becker, op.cit.; interview, Samples, op.cit.; and interview, Lyle, op.cit.

— *Four*—

WOMEN IN
LAW ENFORCEMENT

Women began to enter police work in the late nineteenth and early twentieth centuries in response to the increase in social problems involving women that was beyond the interest or ability of men alone to deal with. Fundamental changes in urban life, especially the impact of immigration and industrialization, vastly increased the amount of crime by women and thus the number of women arrested and incarcerated. the nineteenth century saw a steady and marked rise in the arrest rates of women and girls for prostitution, disorderly conduct, drunkenness, and vagrancy. As the incidence of crime by females increased, a need was felt for some sort of womanly presence in the police station; eventually this presence was extended even to the scene of the crime or arrest, and women truly became integrated into police work.

HISTORICAL BACKGROUND

As with corrections work, women became involved with law enforcement through the various social reform movements that sought to help fallen women regain a respectable place in the home and community. As early as 1820, women had begun to replace clergymen as leaders in the crusade against sexual sin. By 1838 there were approximately 250 local groups of the Female Moral Reform Society in cities in the northeast. By the end of the century, the Women's Prison Association, the Women's Christian Temperance Union, and other women's groups would enter the reform crusade. Although they were concerned with homeless and drunken women, their prime interest centered on eliminating prostitution.[1]

By the mid-nineteenth century, prostitution increased drastically, partly due to conditions resulting from the Civil War and partly from poverty. During the Civil War, women were attracted to the military zones for financial reasons. Many war widows were left homeless, without any means of support. Some became prostitutes, as did a growing number of poor women in the cities.[2]

In Chicago in the 1860s there were 500 brothels filled with thousands of poor young women. In New York there were an estimated 6,000 prostitutes. They usually were young, between 18 and 25, and mostly immigrants. There were guides to the brothels in New York, Philadelphia, Baltimore, Washington, D.C., Boston, and Chicago. Since these guides listed only the upper-class brothels, the actual number of houses and prostitutes can never be known.[3]

By the early twentieth century, prostitution, along with drunkenness and vagrancy, had become the major reasons for the arrest and incarceration of women. Reformers were eager both to convert sexual sinners to morality and to protect arrested and incarcerated women from physical and sexual abuse. They also were concerned about the thousands of homeless women who were housed temporarily in police stationhouses each year. They urged local governments to hire police matrons to supervise women in the stationhouses and recommended separation of incarcerated persons by sex.[4]

In 1845, one year after the creation of the New York City Police Department, the Women's Prison Association and the American Female Moral Reform Society succeeded, after much opposition, in persuading the city to hire six matrons to supervise sentenced and detained girls and women in the jails. It was the first time a U.S. municipality hired matrons, and it set a precedent. In Portland, Maine, for example, members of the Women's Christian Temperance Union had been accustomed to visit women in jails and detention centers, and accompanied them to court to protect them from abuse by men. They regarded this service so highly that they hired and paid women "visitors" for these functions. This group and other women's organizations encouraged the city to provide the funds for the visitors; in 1878, Portland hired police matrons.[5]

However, there was much opposition to having women as police matrons in the stationhouses. Police departments and men's reform groups argued that the women would be "contaminated and demoralized by contact with such depraved creatures" as prostitutes, vagrants, and alcoholics; certainly no "decent, sober, respectable women" would take the job.[6] The reformers, arguing that police matrons were necessary to prevent sexual abuse and attacks upon arrested and incarcerated women by policemen and prisoners, and to protect young girls and first offenders from hardened women criminals, pressed for full-time positions for police matrons. The national, state, and local chapters of the Federation of Women's Clubs, the Young Women's Christian Association, the Women's Christian Temperance Union, and local Protective Leagues for Women and Girls addressed themselves to the need for women in law enforcement. Support for their position was given at the 1886 National Conference of Charities and Corrections.[7]

By 1885 there were police matrons in 11 other cities. In 1888 New York and Massachusetts passed laws requiring cities with a population of over 20,000 to hire police matrons to supervise arrested and detained women. These were political appointments, and it was not uncommon for a woman to be hired upon the death of her policeman husband. Such was the case of Marie Owen. In 1893, after the death of her husband, the mayor of Chicago appointed her to the detective bureau. During her 30-year tenure, her duties were traditional and limited to working with women and children, visiting in courts, and assisting men in detective cases dealing with women and children.[8]

The police matron movement coincided with the professionalization of social work, and many women applied social work concepts and methods to their matron duties. They interviewed and wrote case histories; they went to court and made recommendations regarding setences based on their case studies. In effect, they acted as probation officers to the court and many were so appointed. As probation officers to women released by the courts, they counseled and assisted them in acquiring clothing, housing, and employment.[9]

By the end of the nineteenth century many reformers, recognizing the need for women with full police powers to work outside the stationhouse, began pushing for the appointment of women professionals who would work in the streets with prostitutes, runaways, and delinquents. The first steps were taken in Portland, Oregon in 1905. During the Lewis and Clark Exposition Lola Baldwin, secretary of the Travelers' Aid Society, was hired to protect women and girls from the miners, lumbermen, and laborers attending the event, and to prevent the women and girls from approaching the men. Baldwin, called a "safety worker," was empowered to arrest men and women for illegal acts (although it was the women and girls who were arrested for prostitution, and the girls who were detained for being runaways).[10]

After the Exposition, Portland's city government gave official approval to her work by organizing a Department of Public Safety for the Protection of Young Girls and Women. Baldwin was appointed director.

Neither she nor the police department wanted women to be called policewomen because neither wished to associate women with the concept or job of policemen. The women, called operatives or safety workers, considered themselves social service workers.

The fact that Baldwin held her post throughout the administrations of five mayors and six chiefs of police indicates that she was well thought of, did a good job, and did not go beyond her assigned task.[11] Her career was typical of those women who pioneered in law enforcement. She worked for a social reform organization that focused on protecting and caring for women and children. When she transferred from the organization to the police department, she kept the role of a social worker for women and children. She did not see herself as a cop.

POLICEWOMEN: THEORY AND PRACTICE

The title policewoman first went to Alice Stebbins Wells in Los Angeles in 1910. Wells, a graduate of a theological seminary, was a social worker who dealt with women and children in trouble with the law. She believed that if a woman was invested with police powers she could be of more help than if she worked through a private reform or charity agency. Accordingly, she acquired the signatures of 100 people in reform and in social work and asked the mayor to appoint her as a policewoman with full powers of policing. On September 13, 1910, she received her appointment.[12]

Her appointment received wide publicity and elicited both favorable and hostile comments. She was caricatured in the press in an unflattering manner: a muscular woman wearing glasses, her hair in a bun, and carrying a gun. Policemen did not want her nor did they know what to do with her. On the other hand, the idea of having someone in policing dedicated to helping women and children brought praise from many women's groups.[13]

Wells believed that a woman performed a special task in policing. She

> engages public interest in police crime prevention and commits police departments to it as a recognized and growing part of police duty.... As there existed inherently, though unfilled, a real place for women police officers, without whom a protective work for women, children, and the home could not be developed, both the public and the Police Department accepted the innovation as right and needful.[14]

Her concept of the role of women in policing was the accepted one until the 1960s.

Wells and subsequent policewomen espoused the prevention/protection theory. Their primary function was to prevent women and children from becoming delinquent and to protect them from becoming victims of crime. They focused on women and children, and they operated in a separate women's bureau within the police department.

They acquired their positions as policewomen and were accepted by the police departments and the community because of their stated theory and focus and because they carried out their duties effectively. Their success was the start of a nationwide movement to hire policewomen in all police departments. Wells spoke to women's and civic groups in 75 cities throughout the country, urging that women be hired as policewomen. Although all police departments around the nation did not heed her urgent request, by 1915, at least 16 cities had hired full-time policewomen with pay.[15]

World War I was a turning point for career policewomen. Mobilization resulted in the concentration of large groups of men, mostly young men away from home for the first time, and brought about an increase in the number of women and girls attracted to the servicemen for patriotic, romantic, and financial reasons. The government created zones around military bases where houses of prostitution and sale of alcohol were forbidden and, along with private agencies, funded local reform committees that organized to protect servicemen and to detain and supervise prostitutes and runaways. The women working on these protective committees were given police powers: they went out on patrol, supervising public places where women and girls could congregate and get into trouble, such as transportation depots, amusement areas, and rooming houses; they supervised detention centers for arrested women and girls, and acted as probation officers. By the end of 1918, 198 women were involved in such protective work. One of these women was Ellen O'Grady, the first woman administrator in a police department, who was appointed deputy policy commissioner in charge of the Welfare Bureau for New York City in 1918. There she implemented the protection and prevention theory in dealing with women and children.[16]

After World War I policewomen were at work in more than 210 cities, usually in separate Women's Bureaus. Their duties focused on specialized areas of juvenile delinquency, female victims of sex offenses, women criminal suspects, abandoned infants, missing persons, vice squads, matron duty, and clerical work. A few women were assigned to high risk jobs in detective bureaus that involved investigating and apprehending persons suspected of being involved in vice, gambling, and organized crime. As a rule policewomen received lower salaries than men, had to meet stricter qualifying standards, got little or no training, and were seldom promoted.[17]

The story of New York City's policewomen is typical. This department has had the largest number of policewomen and has kept annual reports that date from the end of the nineteenth century. In addition, many New York policewomen have written books and articles on their work. In 1920, New York State passed a law officially establishing the position of policewomen in New York City, and in 1921 the city gave the first civil service examination for it. Many women, including Adele Priess and Mary Hamilton, who had been appointed policewomen during World War I, took the examination and became official members of the department.[18]

A policewoman had to be a U.S. citizen between 21 and 35 years of age, have a high school diploma, and pass written, oral, and physical examinations. Experience in probation, working with reforming women and minors, teaching, or nursing was desirable. She would earn $1,769 a year and her duties would involve the "moral protection of women and minors; the prevention of delinquency among women and minors; and the performance of such other duties as the Police Commissioner may assign." In contrast, the civil service requirements for policemen mentioned neither education nor work experience, and did not specify a job focus.[19]

In 1921 a separate Bureau of Women was established under the directorship of Mary Hamilton. At first the bureau was located in an abandoned stationhouse, physically separate from any police station. Called the Women's Precinct, it was in a poverty stricken, high crime area known as Hell's Kitchen. The women transformed the "dingy dirty rat hole" into a clean, decorated center that had a clubhouse atmosphere. They provided a hospitable place for troubled women and children to get help from other women, and a place to detain runaway girls. The precinct, said Hamilton, was the "very essence of the principles for which the modern policewomen should stand."[20]

Policewomen also went on patrol, usually in plain clothes rather than in uniform, watching women, especially girls and children, in order to protect them from harm. Hamilton believed it was particularly important to save runaway girls because "every girl whether good or bad is a potential mother and in her rests the hope of the next generation."[21]

The Women's Precinct closed after a short period of time, partly for political reasons, and because the legality of detaining women and girls in the Women's Precinct was questioned. The Bureau of Women was transferred to police headquarters and women were assigned to police precincts to act as matrons if women or children were being held, or for specific assignments.

Federal law enforcement agencies did not hire women, nor did most state agencies until the 1960s. Women began to work for state police departments in 1930 when Massachusetts hired them; Connecticut followed in 1943. In both states they continued to work in special situations dealing with women and children. In federal law enforcement agencies and in states and cities with no policewomen of their own, such women were borrowed from the nearest jurisdiction or hired from private agencies such as the Pinkerton Detective Agency.[22]

Meanwhile, there had appeared a nationally recognized professional organization to represent policewomen in their dealing with policemen and to bring their case to the attention of government and the public. In 1915 Alice Stebbins Wells, the first policewoman, organized the International Association of Police Women (IAPW) and became its first president. The association quickly received the approval of the International Association of Chiefs of Police (IACP), whose president, Richard Sylvester, offered his assistance; in fact, the IACP constitution was used as a model for the women's organization.[23]

As the official voice of policewomen across the country, the IAPW pressed for giving women a separate status within police work so that they could concentrate on the specialized tasks of the social service role and the protection/prevention theory. It noted that women tended to perform certain types of police work, and gave as an example the activities of some Chicago policewomen: returning runaway girls to their homes, warning them of danger from men and loose women, suppressing petty gambling in stores frequented by children, eliminating "dance hall evils" and the sale of alcohol to minors, patrolling railroad depots for runaways and kidnapped children, and securing evidence or conducting investigations in crimes involving women or children.[24]

The IAPW also began to survey police departments to obtain accurate information on the exact situation of policewomen across the country. The first survey was conducted in 1919–20 by the newly elected president, Lieutenant Mina van Winkle, director of the Women's Bureau, Washington, D.C. Police Department. Since many departments did not cooperate in the survey, the results were incomplete; for example, New York City, with the largest number of police matrons, did not respond.[25] At least 146 cities had either police matrons or police women and some had both; salaries ranged from $900 to $2,100 a year. A second survey, conducted in 1925, based on replies from 210 cities, revealed that there were at least 355 police matrons, 395 policewomen, and 22 women who did both jobs; the salaries ranged from $780 to $2,460 a year. The 1925 survey indicated that women now were firmly rooted in careers in policing. Later surveys by other organizations revealed gradual increases in the number of policewomen. In 1950 there were 2,368 and in 1960 there were 5,617, all employed in large urban centers. A 1969 survey by the IACP of 1,330 law enforcement agencies, showed that 34 percent had women working full time and that of the total police force in the nation, women constituted nearly 2 percent.[26]

Opposition to policewomen, originally based on the rationale that no self-respecting woman would want to work with a criminal woman, had gradually ebbed. The first policewomen were a noteworthy group: married, educated, and connected with nationally known women's organizations and causes; their purpose was to work with women and children, so their role was one of social service. As Alice Wells wrote of the theory of police work:

> But we women, and men, who are interested in crime prevention, look more hopefully to the entrance of women into the police field. . . because it first centered and continuously engages public interest in police crime prevention and commits police departments to it as a recognized and growing part of police duty.[27]

Like Baldwin in Portland, the women considered themselves social workers, not cops, and believed they could influence police departments to alter their function from arrest and punishment to prevention and protection. They argued that women were by nature better suited to deal with women and children, that arrested women had the right to have women officers to talk to, and that only women should interview, search, and supervise women and children.

This social service role spilled over into working with juveniles. Many police departments set up separate juvenile divisions and usually assigned women to work with young delinquents. Women used the tools of counseling and casework rather than punishment. In discussing this role, Hamilton said that women would provide "the strong arm of the law as it is expressed in a woman's guiding hand."[28] She advised counseling rather than arrest to avoid stigmatizing the young. However, police-women were not soft and easy with young girls and women. As mothers of the next generation, female offenders were considered dangerous and in need of punishment and reform. Hamilton felt that these young girls and women had to be trained as moral homemakers and that police-women were obligated to perform that task.[29]

Equating police work with social work facilitated the acceptance of women as professionals; they neither competed with men nor claimed the same goals and duties. Rather, women articulated the idea that they were different from men and so could perform certain tasks better than men because those tasks fit their natural capacities and tendencies. Thus policewomen were accepted by men in police departments, by the public, and by social reformers. In 1919, for example, Richard Enright, commissioner of police in New York City, said he considered their work an "absolute necessity" in matters concerning women and children.[30] Louis Brownlow, a reformer, said that policewomen were social workers with a "devotion to mankind."[31] He believed that women would uplift the morals and standards of police departments.

To be sure, policewomen also went out on patrols upon occasion, but invariably in capacities that were consistent with their presumed natural abilities. They were used most frequently as decoys in investigations of rape, abortion, and prostitution. However, until the 1960s, women's role in policing remained unchanged. Most of their work continued to be performed in the stationhouses and in central headquarters, and continued to focus on women and children. Policewomen performed matron duties: searching, questioning, guarding, and escorting women and children to and from courts. They searched women who were dead on arrival at the stationhouses or a hospital. When babies or children were lost or had to be taken to courts or shelters, policewomen took care of them and escorted them wherever necessary.[32]

DISCRIMINATION

These traditional tasks were accepted by most policewomen, who perceived themselves as social workers, more skilled and intelligent than policemen. They also enjoyed more regular hours and usually worked during the day. But there also were severe restrictions in opportunities for those women. The number of women in police departments were kept low by quotas, usually 1 percent, and by job requirements that were higher for them than for men, such as a high school diploma and often college education and work experience. In New York City, educational requirements for men were not stated in civil service announcements until 1955.[33]

Because policewomen did women's work, they were trained differently than policemen, which put them at a disadvantage in the physical aspects of police duty, and did not move along the same course of promotions. In 1952 several New York City policewomen applied to take the competitive examination for the rank of sergeant, but were refused because, according to the civil service job description, the only rank and grade for women was that of policewoman. Then in 1961 policewoman Felicia Shpritzer applied to take the examination. She too was refused by the Civil Service Commission, but this time the matter went to court.[34]

Shpritzer had made a career of law enforcement work. In 1938, when she found that her B.A. and M.A. degrees were no help in getting a job, an experience shared by many men and women during the Depression, she along with approximately 240 other college graduates took the examination for entrance into the police department. She entered in 1942 and, like most college-educated policewomen, was assigned to the Juvenile Aid Division. There she became friends with Gertrude Schimmel, a Phi Beta Kappa from Hunter College who entered the department in 1940 because she could not find a teaching job. She and Shpritzer served in the juvenile division, where they each waited more than 20 years for their first promotion. They had watched many of the men who entered with them in the early 1940s receive promotions and move on to higher salaries and benefits, larger pensions, and jobs with greater status and responsibility. Schimmel later observed: "The veterans among us also knew that to have been deprived of the right to promotion through the years was a grievous, irreparable injury. There would be no restitution for the tremendous career losses that had been sustained."[35]

Their waiting was finally rewarded in 1961, when Shpritzer's suit against the commissioner of Civil Service (*Shpritzer v. Lang*) was decided in her favor by the New York Supreme Court. Nevertheless, the city and the police department denied her right to promotion while they appealed the case. In 1962 the appellate division voted in favor of Shpritzer, but the city and police still refused to budge. Finally, in 1963, another appellate court voted in favor of Shpritzer, and the police and city relented. It had taken two years, three court cases, and 13 judges to convince them that women deserved the equal right to promotion. In 1964 Shpritzer and Schimmel took the examination for sergeant and passed.[36]

As sergeants, Shpritzer and Schimmel were assigned to take turns supervising the women in the Bureau of Policewomen. They continued in this position even after passing the promotion examination for lieutenant, and Schimmel worked there even when in 1971 she became the first woman captain in police history. Late in 1971 Schimmel made history again when she became the first woman to become deputy inspector.[37]

Commissioner Patrick Murphy, who had entered the department in 1940 at the same time as Schimmel, ceased to talk to Shpritzer and Schimmel after they became sergeants and never truly accepted women as equals in the department. In his book *Commissioner: A View From the Top of American Law Enforcement*, he wrote:

> My pet wish is to pass over as quickly as possible the demonstration that women officers can do everything as well as men (et cetera, et cetera) and move to a more intelligent level of discussion and personnel deployment where women are used for the special capabilities they possess.[38]

Their promotion was greeted more positively in 1967 by the new commissioner of police, Howard Leary, who considered the women extremely bright, capable, and tough.[39]

In large part, the victories of Shpritzer and Schimmel were possible because during the 1960s the federal courts and Congress gave legal form to the great movements for civil rights. In 1971 the U. S. Supreme Court, in *Reed* v. *Reed*, declared that any state law discriminating on the basis of sex violates the equal protection clause of the Fourteenth Amendment. This decision was reinforced in *Frontiero* v. *Robinson* when the U. S. Supreme Court decided that sex, as race, is a characteristic that must be justified if used as a classification of people for legislative purposes. In 1972 Title VII of the Civil Rights Act of 1964 was amended to extend the regulatory powers of the Equal Employment Opportunity Commission (EEOC) to cover all governmental agencies on all levels. Title VII prohibits discrimination on the basis of sex, race, color, creed, or national origin by private and union employers. The 1972 amendments require EEOC to examine discriminatory practices in public as well as private employment areas, including local, state, and federal government departments.[40]

More legislation followed. The Crime Control Acts of 1973 and 1976 amended the Omnibus Crime Control and Safe Streets Act of 1968, which had created the Law Enforcement Assistance Administration, the funding agency in the Department of Justice that provides financial assistance for improving law enforcement agencies in the nation. Approximately 40,000 police departments, courts, and correctional facilities receive nearly one billion dollars each year from LEAA. The Crime Control Act of 1973 prohibits sex discrimination against women in employment situations in any agency receiving LEAA aid. The 1976 amendment prohibits LEAA from funding any agency, local, state, or federal, that discriminates against women or other designated groups, and directs that if discriminatory practices are found, their LEAA funds must be terminated.[41]

Women now could enter law enforcement agencies on all three levels of government. They could step beyond traditional roles for women in policing and apply for all positions in law enforcement, receiving the same salaries, promotion opportunities, and benefits as men. In 1974 the number of women on patrol increased from approximately a dozen to almost 1,000; several hundred women were promoted to sergeant, lieutenant, or captain, and assigned to supervise men and women. In 1972 Pennsylvania became the first state to hire women on a state level and to give men and women law officers the same duties. Women are now

members of the state police force in Pennsylvania, Michigan, New
Jersey, and California. In 1978, an estimated 2.7 percent, or 2,024
women, were on state police forces totaling 74,979.[42]

On the federal level, women entered the Executive Protective
Service in 1960, the Secret Service in 1971, and the Federal Bureau of
Investigation in 1972. Thereafter they joined other federal law enforcement agencies such as the Alcohol, Tobacco, and Firearms Administration, and the Drug Enforcement Administration.

Cities followed the same path. In 1972 New York City, the largest
police department with the largest number of women, responded to the
combination of legal, moral, and financial pressures by training women
for patrol duty. In 1973 the Civil Service Commission announced the first
unisex examination for the position of police "officer" (the job title
denotes the unisex intent). By 1974 there were over 700 women in the
department. Men and women take the same qualifying examination,
participate in the same training, are assigned from the same eligibility list
to the same precincts and patrol duties, and are promoted according to the
same standards. The Bureau of Policewomen has been disbanded.[43]
Women have been assigned to the Homicide Divisions, and in 1976
Captain Vittoria Renzullo became the first woman to be in charge of a
police precinct.

Since 1970 women also have been integrated in other cities,
including Los Angeles, Cleveland, Arlington, Dayton, Madison, Dallas
Peoria, Miami, Indianapolis, and Washington, D. C. The degree of
integration depends on whether the department voluntarily accepts
women or is forced to accept them due to pressure from the legislature or
through legal decisions. Police Foundation reports from these cities show
women can perform assigned tasks, including patrol, but there remains
"a significant amount of prejudice against women within police departments."[44]

Case studies in 1970 and 1974 indicated that although women are
being hired and assigned to patrol work, they are not really accepted by
the men in the departments. According to the 1970–71 survey of 60 of the
largest police departments in the nation and in-depth analysis of seven
cities (Philadelphia, New York, Miami, Peoria, Dallas, Washington,
D.C., and Indianapolis), most police departments have quotas of less than
1 percent for women and they have to meet higher educational standards
than men. Women also have to meet weight, height, and physical
examination standards based on male standards. Often there are separate
examinations and separate hiring lists for women, and sometimes they
can be hired only if a woman's slot is vacant. Once hired they receive little
or no training. Special investigatory assignments usually involve vice,
juveniles, or female sex victims, and the clerical work load is heavy. The

1974 report shows little change in the nature of these assignments. Often the women were placed in separate bureaus.[45]

Resistance to women continues both in an overt and covert manner. For example, in New York City policemen fought vigorously to prevent the posting of all openings in the department. Word-of-mouth posting or locker-room posting had guaranteed that only men would hear of certain opportunities and that women would be kept out of certain supervisory positions or special assignments. Ann Powers, president of the Police-women's Endowment Association (PEA), has spoken of the constant struggle of New York City policewomen for equal opportunity. Citing her own experiences, she related how she was sent alone on patrol to a high crime area as punishment for demanding the right for women to go on patrol. Currently assigned to the polygraph division, she claims she is given more work to do than men in order to keep her too busy to conduct her work as president of the PEA. However, she did persuade the department to assign a woman to the Homicide Division in the Detective Bureau and obtained a new contract in 1978 that gave policewomen the same rights and opportunities as men.[46]

One of the reasons most frequently cited by male officers for their reluctance to have women on patrol duties is the fear that women are simply not strong enough for the job. In such physical duty, the men argue, women are vulnerable to being overpowered and injured, perhaps even raped. The efforts of male officers to assist them would limit the effectiveness of the men. In a 1977 study of a class in the Michigan State Police Academy training program, it was found that although the women passed the course, which included physical training, and were respected by the men, they were considered by the men not to be strong enough physically to be desirable as duty partners.[47]

Aside from the degree to which the physical strength issue may affect confidence in women's ability, the strength and agility examinations required by all police departments have formed major barriers to the entrance of women recruits. The state training academy in New Jersey reported that in 1977 and 1978, no women passed their physical agility course, which included running, jumping, shooting, boxing, and judo. Another department test includes walking the balance beam and dragging a 180-pound dummy for 50 feet against a stopwatch. Since 1975, when New Jersey agreed to hire women and minority members in the state police, only two women have been hired as of January 1980.[48]

It is not uncommon for local police departments either to introduce physical agility tests or, in the name of unisex policy, to revise the physical agility tests to make them more difficult. Toni Plantamura sued the Paramus, New Jersey Police Department for denying her the right to become a police officer in 1977 when she headed the civil service list. The mayor said the civil service was not involved and that there was no "law that you have to take No. 1."[49] At that time, the officials ordered a new physical agility test, designed so that women would fail. Plantamura, who runs 70 miles a week and is in good physical shape, said the test she had been given included "chinups, pullups, pushups and walking across parallel bars on your arms and then doing dips to the floor and coming back up." She received 96 on her written examination and 58 on the physical examination.[50]

It is doubtful that a woman will be hired in the Trenton, New Jersey Police Department because of their revised physical agility test. The only woman on the force, Emily Bacovin, retired in 1979 after 37 years on the force, the last eight years as a detective in the Youth Division of the Criminal Investigations Unit. Actually, she had been doing the same work for years as a policewoman; her main assignment was with children. To date, no woman has replaced her because the requirements established as a unisex policy in 1972 have made the physical agility test too difficult for women.[51]

Related to the issues of strength and agility are the minimum size and weight requirements found in almost all departments. Early in 1979, Judge Shirley M. Hufstedler of the Ninth U. S. Circuit Court of Appeals wrote the decision that ended a six-year suit brought against the Los Angeles Police Department (LAPD) by Sergeant Franchon Blake and other women in the LAPD to end certain practices, including the height requirement and gender-based job classifications, that discriminated against women.[52]

The situation in Los Angeles is being repeated in most city and state law enforcement agencies. In 1978 Penelope Brace, a veteran of 15 years on the Philadelphia police force, won her lawsuit against the city and became the first woman detective in the city's history. The police department, with the support of Mayor Frank Rizzo, had refused to promote her in 1976 after she passed the examination, and she had to sue the department. The police department tried to intimidate Brace by trying to put her back on foot patrol, claiming all detectives had to have that experience. Despite claims that "big cops" are needed to deter crime, Brace won her case and is presently a detective, but not a welcomed one. One reason why Philadelphia and Los Angeles complied with the Brace and Blake decisions was that in both cases the U. S. Justice Department also sued for violation of the federal law prohibiting the allocation of federal funds through LEAA to any governmental agency that violated antisex discrimination legislation. In the case of Brace and Philadelphia, the Justice Department was withholding four million dollars in LEAA grants.[53]

Even if police departments hire women and have to promote some, they may discriminate in subtle ways. Women are not included in the "old boys" network, and often are ignorant of promotion and transfer opportunities, special assignments, and general gossip. In the New York City Police Department (NYPD), officers of the network who find out about the plush appointments and get them are called "Charley Gets." Women are excluded.[54]

Other forms of harassment occur. When a woman is on patrol but is the only woman on the force or on duty at a given time, she is pulled off her patrol duty when a woman is arrested to perform matron duties. Police women are sent out as decoys to apprehend muggers, rapists, and solicitors of prostitutes. If the backup policemen do not like women officers and are not supportive of their role in policing, they are less likely to respond properly, increasing the chances that women police officers may experience physical harm. At times, women are assigned to special duties in order to remove them from supportive contact with other women in the department or to punish them for demanding equal rights. Policewomen also experience sexual harassment from bosses in the police department, as do women in the private sector. Each woman has to handle that situation on her own.

In departments containing more than one precinct, women have to prove themselves over and over again in each precinct to which they are assigned. Sergeant Joan Pierson of the NYPD reported that it took the 12 women sergeants in the department as of January 1978 at least six months to be accepted in their precincts. Because there are so few women in each department, women tend to be transferred from one tour of duty or special assignment or precinct to another more frequently than men. Each time a woman is transferred she again has to go through the lonely process of proving her ability by working harder than men.[55]

Women who are trying to enter policing also have to contend with the severe budgetary restrictions that have been put into effect since 1975 in many municipalities. In New York City, funding cuts in 1975 reduced the number of women in the department from approximately 750 to 280, although by 1979 the number increased to almost 500. The layoffs were done on the principle of last one in, first one out. Over 500 of the 750 women hired from the first unisex list in 1973 did not have seniority and many were still on probation; they were the first to go. The rehiring took a long time and is still not complete. Deputy Chief Gertrude Schimmel reported that women in the NYPD have not made significant gains in number in the 38 years she has been on the force: in 1979, women totaled 2.2 percent of the uniformed force, a 1 percent increase since 1940.[56]

PERFORMANCE STUDIES

The difficulties placed in the way of women who seek to be officers are mainly products of traditional ideas, not of objective, demonstrable shortcomings or weaknesses. Evaluations of policewomen's effectiveness on patrol have been made in five major studies: Washington, D.C., 1974; St. Louis, Missouri, 1975; California Highway Patrol, 1976; Denver, Colorado, 1977; and New York City, 1977. The reports show that women can perform the duties traditionally assigned to men and just as effectively. They also indicate that men are in no more danger with women as partners than they are with men as partners. In fact, the Washington, D.C. report stated that the presence of women tended to prevent dangerous situations rather than bring them on. The St. Louis study reported similar results: citizen reaction to policewomen was positive and policewomen were perceived as being more polite and sensitive than policemen.[57] In 1977, Commissioner Glen Craig of the California Highway Patrol, said results of a comprehensive study conducted by his department proved that men and women behaved equally well in the job: "Each male and female officer remaining on duty was performing acceptably."[58]

The most extensive report to date is one done in 1978 by the Vera Institute of Justice in New York City. It concluded that women performed as well as men:

> women's "style" of patrol was almost indistinguishable from the men's... citizens rated the female officers more competent, pleasant and respectful than their male counterparts... there was no evidence of difference between male and female officers' behavior in the few incidents where civilians were agitated or where there were other indications of danger.[59]

Perhaps equally important, the study revealed that policewomen received fewer patrol duties than men because they had to guard women prisoners, and when they were on patrol they were "less often assigned to ride with the same patrol partner; they therefore had less opportunity to gain knowledge of their precincts and of the ground rules for participating with a partner in patrol functions."[60] The constant shifting of policewomen from one precinct to another and from one assignment to another prevents them from becoming part of a team, and prevents policemen from understanding the strengths of their female partners.

One of these strengths is in dealing with victims of rape and battering. The victims of these assaults tend to view policemen as members of the aggressor group, but policewomen are not seen this way.

Women officers also are able to go into the examining room with the victim and observe firsthand the physical evidence of attack and immediately receive from the doctor any specimens or statements of a medical nature about the injuries of the victim. Thus the policewoman is able to act as a witness should the assaulter be apprehended and go to trial. On the whole, women are likely to treat women victims and offenders more sympathetically; this is a matter of agreement among all researchers. Cynthia Sultan, project director of the Police Foundation's study on the role of policewomen, has also observed that women officers usually are willing to let prisoners with children make phone calls home.[61]

DIVISION OVER GOALS

The emphasis on integration of the sexes has helped change the nature of much police work done by women. Traditionally, policewomen were the specialists, working with juveniles, children, and other women. The more recent entrants are more likely to be generalists who take part in all phases of police work. Since the generalists see themselves as policewomen above all, they do not perceive themselves as social service workers typical of most policewomen before the 1960s. By and large the mothering aspect of women's police work has disappeared. Sergeant Carolen Bailen of the St. Paul Police Department said at the 1971 meeting of the International Association of Women Police that specialization was too limiting and that women should participate in all aspects of law enforcement. Other policewomen voiced regret over this change. Inspector Dorothy Gay of the Detroit Women's Bureau and Lois Higgens, Chicago juvenile officer, saw patrol duty as a demotion from the kind of specialized work they were used to doing, and believed that women should continue to be specialists.[62]

Along with the demise of the mothering concept, there has been an increasing emphasis on the tangible rewards of a law enforcement career. Pay, promotions, and pensions have become major issues. Cynthia Sultan of the Police Foundation, on the basis of her visits to police departments around the nation, has concluded that policewomen who entered after 1970 are different from those who entered before that date. Today's women have a law enforcement mentality, not a social service orientation; their attitudes, career goals, and behavior more closely resemble men's.[63]

However, she observed, women enter at the lower level, and have been conditioned to see their place in policing at that lowest level. The perceived limit on mobility affects their attitude and behavior. They have low morale and become depressed with the restrictions on them, both real and imagined. Several officers, especially those in cities with a single precinct and only a small number of officers, have said they might leave policing because the political and bureaucratic nature of the department will make promotion difficult.[64]

Despite these conditions, police work has an appeal for college-educated women, especially those in areas of high unemployment. For women not so well educated, and for educated minority women who find their color or ethnic origin a hindrance to good employment in business and industry, police work has acquired a growing attraction. The starting salary in the NYPD in 1979 was $15,500, and in three years it increased to $18,500, with the benefits of pension, sick and maternity leaves, and vacation time included. There are not too many jobs in the private sector where women, black or white, can receive that salary and such benefits with only a high school education and no special skills. Marjorie L. Lewis, a veteran of 20 years on the force, became the first black woman to become sergeant in 1971. Although she has a college education, she explained that she was concerned with job security and a good salary, and felt that as a black woman she could best attain these goals in the civil service environment of policing.[65]

THE FUTURE

The general picture that emerges out of this examination of women in law enforcement is that after enormous effort, women have obtained significant changes in law, a few changes in practice, and little change in the outlook of most male police. The future probably will bring more of the same. Because of the fear of legal action by women or women's groups that could lead to the loss of LEAA funds, police departments, when pressured, will revise their laws and allow women to take the entrance examinations. However, most women will fail to pass the physical agility test. On paper and from examples of individual women, it will appear that women are equal with men; but for reasons already mentioned, this will not be a reality for most policewomen.

The number of policewomen almost certainly will continue to rise, but at what rate is debated by researchers. In 1977, 10,381 women comprised 2.7 percent of the total law enforcement officers in the nation's cities and local municipalities. On a state level, 2,024 women comprised .03 percent of the force. On a federal level, 2 percent of the FBI and 2 percent of the Secret Service are women; a total in all federal law enforcement agencies of 1,591 women. It is estimated that out of a total of

518,326 law officers in the United States, 13,996 are women.[66] Almost all of the women are employed in urban areas and work in only 50 percent of the total number of police departments in the nation. The International Association of Chiefs of Police studied the number and performance of policewomen and reported that about 1,644 policewomen went on patrol in 375 departments, but that the majority of women continued to be assigned to traditional roles in policing.[67] Catherine Milton of the Police Foundation, Theresa Melchionne, professor at John Jay College of Criminal Justice, and Peter Horne, professor at St. Louis Community College, predict that women will compose 10 to 50 percent of department personnel by the year 2000. The author sees a slight increase, perhaps 10 percent, and continuation of the traditional policewomen roles.[68]

Budget considerations, particularly if the present citizen tax revolt continues and veterans' preference laws also will work against women in the future. Fewer will be hired and small numbers will affect their assignments. Some women probably will be transferred from patrol duty to matron duty. Only when the matron duties and other women's police jobs are filled (such as working with juveniles, women offenders, and rape victims and doing decoy work in vice squads) will women be assigned to patrol work.

Economic factors and veterans' preference laws limiting the number of women hired will keep low the number of women being promoted to administrative positions. It will take many years for them to accumulate the experience and seniority needed for promotions or appointments to top advisory positions in police departments. New York City with its woman deputy chief inspector and assistant commissioner is unique. As Schimmel said at a meeting of the New York Women in Criminal Justice on January 18, 1979, "women are not doing well in the Department."[69]

Ironically, women's attitudes concerning the special capacities of women also will keep them in traditional roles. Women's groups want women officers on task forces for rape and battering victims. Police administrators may yield (with pleasure) to these pressures and assign policewomen to "specialization of the patrol function," that is, to traditional work.[70] In other words, just as there is a call for minority men to deal with minority offenders, there is a call for women to work with women victims and offenders; but minority men become part of the "old boys" network, whereas women remain outsiders.

It is only 17 years since Felicia Shpritzer won the first lawsuit against a police department giving her permission to take a promotion examination, setting the example for others to follow. However, lawsuits have to be brought woman by woman, department by department, on local, state, and federal levels, and that takes a very long time. Many men in law enforcement and many people in the community still believe as did

Raymond Fosdick, reformer in law enforcement in the early twentieth century: "When policewomen put on uniforms and carried guns and clubs, they became little men, but when they did their work as women, they rendered a great service."[71]

NOTES

1. David J. Pivar, *Purity Crusade: Sexual Morality and Social Control, 1868–1900* (Westport, Conn.: Greenwood Press, 1973), pp. 26–27.

2. Estelle B. Freedman, "Their Sisters' Keepers: An Historical Perspective on Female Correctional Institutions in the United States: 1870–1900," *Feminist Studies* 2 (1974): 82.

3. Pivar, op.cit., pp. 31–32.

4. Theresa M. Melchionne, "Policewomen: Their Introduction into the Police Department of the City of New York" (Masters Thesis, Bernard M. Baruch School of Business and Public Administration of CUNY, 1961), pp. 1–24.

5. Ibid., pp. 4–6; and Chloe Owings, *Women Police: A Study of the Development and Status of the Women Police Movement* (1925; reprint ed., Montclair, N.J.: Patterson Smith, 1969), pp. 97–99.

6. Theresa M. Melchionne, "The Changing Role of Policewomen," in *The Ambivalent Force: Perspectives on the Police,* ed. Arthur Niederhoffer and Abraham S. Blumberg (Hinsdale, Ill.: Dryden Press, 1976), pp. 370–71.

7. Owings, op.cit., p. 97; and Pivar, op.cit., p. 103.

8. Owings, op.cit., pp. 98–100.

9. Ibid., pp. 134–35.

10. Ibid., pp. 99–101; and Melchionne, "Policewomen: Their Introduction," op.cit., pp. 4–5.

11. Owings, op.cit., pp. 100–1.

12. Alice S. Wells, "Twenty and Two Years a Police Woman," *Western Woman* 7 (July–September 1932): 15–16; and "Reminiscences of a Policewoman," *Police Reporter* September 1929): 23–28; George D. Wilson, "The World's First," *L. A. Police Beat* 27 (February 1972): 7, and Owings, op.cit., pp. 101–4.

13. Wells, "Twenty and Two Years," op. cit., p. 15; and "Reminiscences," op. cit., pp. 23–28; and Owings, op.cit., pp. 102–3.

14. Wells, "Twenty and Two Years," op. cit., p. 15.

15. Ibid.; Wells, "Reminiscences," op.cit., pp. 25–28; and Owings, op.cit., pp. 103–4 and 106.

16. Owings, op. cit., pp. 107–17; New York City Police Department, *Annual Report 1918,* p. 85; and *1919,* p. 124.

17. Owings, op.cit., pp. 120–22, and 223–46; Melchionne, "Policewomen: Their Introduction," op.cit., pp. 96–98 and 110–11; Wells, "Twenty and Two Years," op.cit., p. 16; and Mary E. Hamilton, *The Police Woman: Her Service and Ideals* (1924; reprint ed., New York: Arno Press and the New York Times, 1971), pp. 16–18.

18. Hamilton, op.cit., pp. 18–21; and Melchionne, "Policewomen: Their Introduction," op.cit., pp. 94 and 110–13.

19. Hamilton, op.cit., pp. 18–21; and Melchionne, op.cit., pp. 110–13.

20. Hamilton, op.cit., pp. 57–59.

21. Ibid., pp. 111–12.

22. Lois L. Higgins, *Policewoman's Manual* (Springfield, Ill.: Charles C. Thomas, 1961), p. xvi; and Peter Horne, *Women in Law Enforcement* (Springfield, Ill.: Charles C. Thomas, 1974), pp. 17 and 22.

23. Owings, op.cit., pp. 104–5; Wells, "Twenty and Two Years," op.cit., p. 15; and "Reminiscences," op.cit., p. 28.

24. Owings, op.cit., pp. 191–200; and William J. Bopp and Donald O. Schultz, *A History of American Law Enforcement* (Springfield, Ill.: Charles C. Thomas, 1972), p. 82.

25. Owings, op.cit., pp. 119–22.

26. Ibid.; and Catherine Milton, *Women in Policing* (Washington, D.C.: Police Foundation, 1972), pp. 7 and 16.

27. Wells, "Twenty and Two Years," op.cit., p. 15; and Owings, op.cit., pp. 105 and 261–63.

28. Hamilton, op.cit., p. 183; Felicia Shpritzer, "Major Administrative Problems of the Police Department in the Shelter and Detention of Minors" (Masters thesis, Bernard M. Baruch School of Business and Public Administration of CUNY, 1961), pp. 1–123; and Owings, op.cit., pp. 205–22.

29. Hamilton, op.cit., pp. 153–57.

30. New York City Police Department, *Annual Report 1919*, p. 167.

31. Higgins, op.cit., pp. xvii–xviii.

32. Ibid., pp. 3 7; Hamilton, op.cit., pp. 67–73, 89–102, and 105–12; Shpritzer, op.cit., pp. 9–21; and Milton, op.cit., pp. 8–9.

33. Milton, op.cit., pp. 16–19; and Municipal Reference Library, New York City, "Civil Service Announcement Folder, Civil Service Examination Announcement, 1955."

34. Felicia Shpritzer, "A Case for the Promotion of Policewomen in the City of New York," *Journal of Criminal Law, Criminology and Police Science* 50 (December 1959): 417; Milton, op.cit., p. 73; and interviews, Felicia Shpritzer, former lieutenant, New York City Police Department, June 27, 1978, and July 5, 1978.

35. Interviews, Shpritzer, op.cit.; interview, Theresa M. Melchionne, former detective and deputy commissioner in charge of community relations, New York City Police Department, January 3, 1978; quoted in Catherine Milton, et. al., *Women in Policing: A Manual* (Washington, D.C.: Police Foundation, 1974), p. 27.

36. Interviews, Shpritzer, op.cit.

37. Ibid.; and Milton, op.cit., p. 73.

38. Patrick V. Murphy and Thomas Plate, *Commissioner: A View from the Top of American Law Enforcement* (New York: Simon and Schuster, 1977), p. 249.

39. Interview, Howard Leary, former commissioner, New York City Police Department, March 6, 1979.

40. Milton et al., pp. 49–51.

41. Ibid.

42. Ibid., p. v; and Peter Horne, "Policewomen: 2000 A.D." (paper presented at the Annual Meeting of the Academy of Criminal Justice Sciences, 1979) p. 4.

43. Horne, "Policewomen: 2000 A.D." op.cit., p. 4; Melchionne, "The Changing Role of Policewomen," op.cit., p. 376; Deirdre Carmody, "The Police Divided Over Assignment of Women to Street Patrol Here," *New York Times*, July 15, 1974, pp. 27 and 38; Leonard Buder, "Police to Put Women on Homicide Squads," *New York Times*, November 16, 1977, p. B3; Murray Schumach, "First Woman Head of Precinct," *New York Times*, December 10, 1976, p. A1; and interview, Ann Powers, president, Policewomen's Endowment Association, July 5, 1978.

44. Milton et al., op.cit., pp. v and 1–5.

45. Ibid., pp. 1–5 and 36–45; and Milton, op.cit., pp. 59–98.

46. Interview, Powers, op.cit.

47. Milton et al., op.cit., pp. 36–45; and Michael T. Charles, "The Performance and Socialization of Female Recruits in the Michigan State Police Training Academy" (Paper presented at the Annual Meeting of the Academy of Criminal Justice Sciences, 1979), pp. 26–27.

48. "Jersey Considering Female-Trooper Test," New York Times, June 30, 1979, p. 22; and May 21, 1978, section 11, pp. 1 and 23.

49. Alfonso A. Narvaez, "Women Seeking a Police Job Sues Paramus, Accusing It of Sex Bias," New York Times, March 30, 1978, p. NJB3.

50. Ibid.

51. Cassandra Lawton, "No Woman Can Fill Her Spot on City Police Force," Sunday Times Advertiser, April 22, 1979, pp. E1 and E8.

52. "Sex Bias Ruling Reversed Major Victory for Women of LAPD," National NOW Times News, June 1979, p. 3.

53. "Woman Officer Very Unhappy with Her Police Job," Bucks County Courier Times, April 20, 1978, p. C40; "Sex-discrimination Trial Resumes After 2-year Break for Police Study," Philadelphia Inquirer, August 15, 1978, section B, p. 1; and "Penelope's Promoted," Trentonian, September 16, 1978, p. 14.

54. Interview, Powers, op.cit.

55. Ibid.; and New York Women in Criminal Justice, Inc., "Minutes of Meeting, January 18, 1979."

56. New York Women in Criminal Justice, op.cit.

57. Peter Block and Deborah Anderson, Policewomen on Patrol: Final Report (Washington, D.C.: Police Foundation, 1974), pp. 5–7; Lawrence J. Sherman, "Evaluation of Policewomen on Patrol in a Suburban Police Department," Journal of Police Science and Administration, 3 (December 1975): 434–38; Women Traffic Officer Project: Final Report (Sacramento, Calif.: Department of California Highway Patrol, 1976); Harold Bartlett and Arthur Rosenblum, Policewomen Effectiveness (Denver, Colo.: Civil Service Commission and Denver Police Department, 1977); and Joyce L. Sichel, et al., Women on Patrol: A Pilot Study of Police Performance in New York City (Washington, D.C.: National Institute of Law Enforcement and Criminal Justice, 1978).

58. Glen Craig, "California Highway Patrol: Women Officers," Police Chief (January 1977): 61.

59. Sichel et al., op.cit., pp. xi–xii.

60. Ibid.

61. Interview, Cynthia Sultan, project director, Police Foundation, June 4, 1979.

62. Milton, op.cit., p. 25; interview, Shpritzer, op.cit.; and interview, Melchionne, op.cit.

63. Interview, Sultan, op.cit.

64. Ibid.

65. "First Black Woman Promoted to Sergeant," New York Times, November 7, 1971, p. 58.

66. Horne, "'Policewomen: 2000 A.D.," op.cit., pp. 3–5.

67. Terry Eisenberg, Police Personnel Practices in States and Local Government (Gaithersburg, Md.: International Association of Chiefs of Police, 1973), p. 39; and Brenda E. Washington, Deployment of Female Police Officers in the United States (Gaithersburg, Md.: International Association of Chiefs of Police, 1974), pp. 1–2.

68. Melchionne, "The Changing Role of Policewomen," op.cit., p. 376; Horne, "Policewomen: 2000 A.D.," op.cit., pp. 6–7; and Catherine Milton, "The Future of Women

in Policing," in *The Future of Policing*, ed. Alvin W. Cohn (Beverly Hills, Calif.: Sage Publications, 1978), pp. 185–87.

69. New York Women in Criminal Justice, op.cit.

70. Horne, "Policewomen: 2000 A.D.," op.cit., p. 18.

71. Hamilton, op.cit., p. 5.

— *Five* —

WOMEN IN THE LEGAL PROFESSION

The development of professions and professionalization that so marked the nineteenth century has left a deep imprint on the practice of law. Professionalization meant the development of generally recognized standards by which competence and ethical conduct could be determined, usually in a peer review process. These standards were drawn up by members of the profession who formed one or more professional organizations that gave a sense of identity and a monolithic public face. Naturally, the prevailing mores and values of the majority of members gave each profession its own character and helped set standards and norms.

As had happened with corrections and law enforcement, so with lawyers; the professionals were almost all men and the professional standards set up were best suited for men and not for women. Women who wanted to practice law on an equal basis with men had to fight many of the same battles as women in corrections and law enforcement. Although female correction officers, policewomen, and women lawyers tend to represent different social and educational levels and might seem to have quite different interests, they also share many common problems.

HISTORICAL BACKGROUND

The first woman in the United States to practice with the approval of the existing political and judicial leadership was Margaret Brent. The provincial court of colonial Maryland admitted her to practice before it in 1648. Among other business, she came before the court concerning the estates of Governor Leonard Calvert and his brother Cecilius. She was not really a lawyer, however, in the sense of one who was trained and officially admitted to the bar. The first woman to meet this criterion in a professional sense was Arabella A. Mansfield, who was admitted to the Iowa bar in 1869.[1]

The reasons that impelled women to enter law were somewhat different from those that drew women to the corrections and law enforcement professions emerging in the nineteenth century. At first, women in corrections and law enforcement began as unpaid reformers or as employees of community service agencies. Even when professionalization set in, the reform aspect remained a major component in both fields, and women who entered the fields often came with a social service background. This altruistic element was not as important for women who entered law, although they often contributed their time and support to needy causes before and after they became lawyers. A common reason for having gone into law was interest spurred by early contact with judges and lawyers; this especially was true for women who came from families where several members were lawyers. Several women entered law as a by-product of the need to handle large inheritances or to handle their own affairs. Finally, there were some whose reform activities led them to realize that poor women needed legal assistance.[2]

Whatever their reasons, women entered law in growing numbers during the nineteenth century. Most of them already had a college education when they went to law school. Women's education was going through a revolution in the United States. Under the leadership of activists such as Hannah Crocker, Emma Willard, Frances Wright, and Catherine Beecher, educational seminaries for girls and teacher-training schools for women opened. Colleges and universities accepted women beginning with Oberlin in 1833 and Antioch in 1852. Iowa was the first state university to accept women; Michigan, Wisconsin, Boston, and Cornell Universities also did in the years from 1858 to 1874. Mount Holyoke, the first women's college, was founded in 1837 by Mary Lyon, Vassar opened in 1865, Smith and Wellesley in 1875, Radcliffe in 1879, and Bryn Mawr in 1885. The American Association of University Women was founded in 1882. By the end of the Civil War, a generation of college-educated women was ready for the next step. For many it was the law.[3]

The very full historical evidence of the nineteenth century makes it impossible to examine all the women who entered law before 1900, which is unfortunate since most of them were remarkable people. But it is possible to select a sample large enough to provide some flavor. Of 39 women lawyers born between 1829 and 1886, 27 were married, 16 to other lawyers. Nine became the law partners of their husbands. In their quest to enter law, all received encouragement from men who were lawyers or judges. Nine actively wrote or lobbied for reforms that assisted women. Only one woman retired from law after marriage. Except for Charlotte Ray, a black woman educated at Howard Law School and admitted to the Washington, D.C. bar in 1872, all the women were white Protestants. Fifteen were in their twenties when they became lawyers; 13 were in their thirties; six were in their forties; and four were in their fifties. Twenty-six lived and practiced in the West, where the first law schools to open to women were located. They were wives and mothers as well as reformers and activists. Using their education and husband's job as indicators, it appears that these women were of the middle and upper classes.[4]

THE LAWYERS

Arabella A. Mansfield, the first woman lawyer in the United States graduated from Iowa Wesleyan Seminary in 1866. She prepared for the bar examination by reading in a private law office. She passed the examination and was admitted to the Iowa bar in June 1869. It is difficult to explain why she was admitted while others that very year and afterwards were denied the privilege. Perhaps it was because she was married to a professor with whom she taught at Iowa Wesleyan; they both applied to be admitted to the bar, and since it seemed they would remain teachers, that may explain why the Iowa court allowed her to be a lawyer. The court reinterpreted a statute providing that admission to the bar be restricted to "white male citizens." The judge, basing his opinion on another section of the statute, said that the use of the word "men" might also be interpreted to include women. He said that restrictive words that treat persons unfairly might be fairly reinterpreted by the courts.[5]

Few other women were received so positively by the courts when they requested admission to the bar. Myra Bradwell studied law in her husband's law office in order to help him with his law practice. In 1869 at the age of 38 she passed the bar examination and then applied to the Illinois Supreme Court for a license to practice. She proved that she was of good character and had met all the requirements for such a license, but the court cited four reasons to refuse her a license. First, under the common-law doctrine of coverture, a married woman did not have the legal right to enter into third-person contracts, and contracts were essential to the lawyer/client relationship. (Under the common-law doctrine of coverture, the husband and wife are to be treated as a single entity; in practice, the single person proved to be the husband.) Second, in the common-law tradition, women never had been lawyers and so the laws of the state of Illinois did not provide for such situations. Third, if women were permitted to practice law, they also might seek the right to hold public office. Fourth, admitting women to the bar would expose them to obscenities in the court trials, threatening their delicacy.[6]

That year Bradwell appealed her case before the U. S. Supreme Court, claiming that her rights were being violated under the equal protection clause of the Fourteenth Amendment. In 1872 the Supreme Court denied her appeal, declaring that the right to practice law was not protected under the Fourteenth Amendment and that states could establish criteria for licensing. In a separate concurring opinion, Justice Joseph P. Bradley claimed that women's domestic role was essential to the preservation of the social order. Although he admitted that not all women married, he did not believe that they had a right to participate in the law. He concluded that the family was founded on "divine ordinance" and that "The paramount mission of women is to fulfill the noble and benign offices of wife and mother. This is the law of the Creator."[7]

Although Bradwell never reapplied for a license to practice law in Illinois, she received one in 1890 by a grant of the state supreme court and became the first woman member of the Illinois Bar Association. She had not been idle during the 21 years between instituting her court case and receiving her license. She was actively involved with gaining the passage of laws to protect women in the state, prevent employment discrimination based on sex, give married women the right to keep their earnings, and guarantee a widow a share in her husband's estate and to provide that same right to widowers. She also founded and edited the *Chicago Legal News*. Her career demonstrated that there was no conflict between marriage, motherhood, and a career. She had children and her daughter became a lawyer.[8]

Although Belva A. Lockwood did not have to wait as long as Bradwell to practice law, she had to overcome other obstacles. Born in 1830, Lockwood graduated from Genesee College, New York, in 1857 and received her Masters degree from Syracuse University in 1870. Columbia College in Washington, D. C., refused to admit her because "her presence in the classes would distract the young men."[9] She was admitted to and graduated from National University Law School in Washington, D.C., and was admitted to the bar in Washington, D.C. in 1873 at the age of 43. Her practice involved litigation against the federal government that required her to plead before the U. S. Supreme Court. She applied in October 1876 and in November the Court denied her the right to practice before it. The Court based its opinion on a common-law precedent that stated that since only men were admitted to the practice of law before the Court, women therefore were excluded. She proceeded to draft a bill enabling women lawyers to practice before the U. S. Supreme Court. In 1879, after three years of lobbying, Congress passed such a law and Lockwood became the first women to practice before the U. S. Supreme Court. She nevertheless was refused admission to the Virginia bar in 1890.[10]

While denying married women the right to be members of the bar or to practice before a specific court was based on coverture, denying single women the right had to rely on a different rationale. The courts believed women must not be encouraged to remain single, to become educated professionals, or to have equal careers with men. Such women were superfluous and unnatural. When R. Lavinia Goodell applied for admission to the Wisconsin Supreme Court in 1875, her request was denied by Chief Justice Edward G. Ryan, who spoke for the court when he declared that no state law had overturned the common-law precedent of refusing to grant women the right to practice law. Recognizing that not all women marry, Ryan declared:

> It is public policy to provide for the sex, not for its superfluous members; and not to tempt women from the proper duties of their sex by opening to them duties peculiar to ours. There are many employments in life not unfit for female character. The profession of the law is surely not one of these.[11]

Ryan believed that women were naturally delicate, emotional, sensitive, and destined by the laws of nature to be mothers and homemakers. Because of these female inadequacies, the client would suffer by not receiving full justice in the hands of a woman lawyer. Women, lacking discretion, could not be trusted to keep a client's information secret as the profession demanded. In addition, exposure to the verbal conflicts in the courtroom would lessen a woman's purity and make her less desirable in the eyes of men.[12]

Lockwood, the first woman to argue before the U. S. Supreme Court, advised women to fight back. Her own career set an example. As an active member of the Woman's National Equal Rights Party in California, she ran for president in 1884 and 1888. She urged women not to be intimidated by public opinion and not to fear moving out of the conforming role of womanhood. She advised women to join forces and make the arduous effort to overcome the discriminatory treatment of women seeking careers in law. Women had to alter opinions so that the public would regard women lawyers as a natural part of the profession. They also had to overcome their own fears of being different and supposedly undesirable as women and potential wives.[13]

Several women heeded her advice and appealed to legislatures to have laws passed to admit women to the profession. Goodell finally became a lawyer with permission to practice before the Wisconsin Supreme Court after the state legislature passed a law granting women that right in 1875. In 1884, Carrie B. Kilgore received the right to practice before the Supreme Court of Pennsylvania by a legislative act. Others went to court to gain entrance into law schools.

It was not until 1920, 51 years after women became lawyers for the first time, that all the states permitted women to practice law before the courts. In 1880, an estimated 75 women and 64,042 men practiced law in the United States. In 1890, the estimated number of women was 135 and by the end of the century it was 300. By 1920 the total number of women who had been admitted to the bar over the past 51 years was an estimated 1,600.[14]

In 1888 the Women's International Bar Association was established, and in 1899 the National Association of Women Lawyers was organized in New York. These groups worked to gain entrance for women to all law schools, to all state bars and courts, and tried to improve the legal status of women in all areas of life. In 1918 the American Bar Association admitted its first women members.[15]

LEGAL EDUCATION

In the nineteenth century many attorneys, women as well as men, received their education and experience in a private law office. Women usually worked and studied with fathers or husbands. By the end of the nineteenth century, however, the professionalization of the law mandated that lawyers have a formal legal education. Phoebe W. Couzens was the first woman to enter a law school. In 1868 she matriculated at Washington University Law School in St. Louis, the first law school to admit women; she graduated in 1871. Subsequently, she was admitted to practice in Missouri, Kansas, Utah, and the U. S. District Courts, became the first woman U. S. marshall (assigned to the eastern district of Missouri), and was actively involved in women's suffrage and prison reform. The credit for being the first woman graduate of a law school goes to Ada Kepley, from Union College in Chicago in 1869.[16]

Of the 39 women lawyers in the sample discussed earlier, 24 graduated from law schools: Boston University, Chicago Union College of Law (now Northwestern University Law School), University of Wisconsin, Hastings College of Law in California, Yale University, Washington University, National University, New York University

(NYU), and the University of Pennsylvania. Some admitted women only under court order, and Yale reverted to an exclusionary policy after admitting Alice Jordan in 1885. Harvard Law School refused to admit Ellen A. Martin and M. Fredrika Perry on the ground that it was not proper for men and women to use the law library at the same time. Carrie Kilgore, denied entrance to the University of Pennsylvania Law School in 1871, went to court and won the right to enter that law school in 1881. The law schools of Yale, Harvard, and Columbia refused women until 1929, when Columbia broke rank and the others followed. The last law school to admit women was Washington and Lee in 1972.[17]

Because of the time and energy involved in gaining admittance to law schools, some women established their own law classes or schools. The Women's Legal Education Society, organized in New York City in 1890, set up the Woman's Law Class of New York University in 1890. Its purpose was to educate women about their rights so that they could protect themselves and other women in need of legal advice. The idea came from Mrs. Leonard Weber, who in 1887 founded the Arbitration Society to aid poor women in need of legal protection. She soon learned that male lawyers did not want to work for poor people who had no money to pay fees. They also did not want to contribute their time free of charge to the Arbitration Society. Weber asked Emily Kempec, a lawyer with a degree from the University of Zurich, to take charge of the legal advice and services of the Arbitration Society. Kempec, as an alien, could not belong to the New York Bar, and thus could not try cases in court.[18]

Weber and Kempec had the cooperation of Henry M. MacCracken, vice-chancellor of New York University. The Woman's Law Class received permission to meet at the NYU law school and Kempec lectured to nonmatriculated women. It is not surprising that MacCracken agreed to cooperate with the women. They were members of the elite, the leaders of the social, educational, and philanthropic communities in New York City. Many were married to politicians and lawyers.[19]

Although men attended Kempec's class on Roman law, they did not recognize her as an official teacher. In fact, the first Woman's Law Class did not pose a threat because most men and most members of the NYU faculty considered it a novelty. Of 15 women in the class, four paid and 11 received scholarships from the Society. At the end of the year of classes, 13 women were tested on their knowledge of the law by MacCracken, Judge Noah Davis, and a partner in the law firm of Solomon, Dullon, and Sutro. (Sutro's wife was a member of the Society.) All thirteen passed and won certificates of graduation; but they were not officially lawyers.[20]

Although newspaper articles about the graduation of the women described their appearance as sweet and lovable, not lawyerlike, the women took their studies seriously and proved to be dedicated students.

In 1892, 57 women enrolled in the Woman's Law Class and the class became a permanent program for women at NYU. In the first four yers of the class, all but one woman went on to law school and two passed the New York bar examination. Three received their Bachelor of Law degrees from NYU in 1893; Katherine Hogan, who passed the bar in 1894; Cornelia Hood, who went on to lecture at the Brooklyn Institute; and Melle Stanleyetta Titus, who became the first woman member of the New York Bar. In the class of 1893, Titus was first in her class of 105 men and five women. She was admitted to the U. S. Circuit Court of Appeals for the New York district.[21]

The women's law school, the Washington College of Law in Washington, D. C., was started by Emma Gillett and Ellen Spencer Mussey. Mussey taught in a business school in Washington, D. C. When her lawyer husband became ill she worked in his law office. Rejected by the local law schools, she read for the law and passed the bar examination. She began practicing law in Washington, D.C. in 1893 at the age of 43, and in 1896 was admitted to practice before the U. S. Supreme Court. She then joined with Gillett to start a law school that would not refuse women (it also admitted men). Gillett had received her degree from Howard University, a black university that admitted women regardless of race. She was admitted to the bar and practiced before the U. S. Supreme Court in 1890. The women became the deans of their new law school, which in 1949 merged with American University.[22]

Both women had political and legal connections in Washington, D.C. that contributed to their success with the law school. Mussey practiced probate, commercial, and international law, and for 25 years was counsel to the Norwegian and Swedish legations. She also was a member of the National American Women Suffrage Association. Gillett was appointed by President James Garfield to be the first woman notary public in Washington, D.C. With a man partner, she practiced probate, realty, and pension law. She also founded the Women's Bar Association of Washington, D. C.[23]

By 1920, 102 of the 129 law schools listed in the Educational Directory of the U. S. Bureau of Education admitted women. Until the 1970s women were accepted in limited numbers to law schools, and only after being questioned about personal life plans such as marriage, children, and career goals. They were asked if they planned to practice law or just look for a husband. Often they were told they were wasting seats in the law school that should go to men who had families to support, or simply that women did not belong in law.[24]

In 1920 Beatrice Doerschuk reported on 297 women in law school and in practice. Women were at a disadvantage for several reasons. As youngsters they were not taught the simple legal and business procedures that boys were. Few women graduated from top schools; women could not get into some of the top law schools and were limited by quotas in others. According to Doerschuk, most of the women who went to law school wanted to become lawyers because they had respect for the law and confidence that they could succeed. However, she estimated that only half of the women who went to law school eventually practiced law. Many were discouraged by discrimination.[25]

Since the 1920s opportunities for a legal education have improved considerably. Women have benefited from Title IX of the Higher Education Act of 1972. Title IX is similar to Title VII of the Civil Rights Act of 1964 in that it forbids discrimination on the basis of sex. It covers student enrollment and faculty hiring, and extends the provisions of the Equal Pay Act of 1963 to cover academic faculty. It provides that any school that discriminates shall be denied federal financial assistance.

The pressure of financial penalties has encouraged law schools to admit more women students and to allow them the opportunity to compete equally with men. The number of women enrolled has tripled between 1969–70 and 1974–75, and increased tenfold from 1966 (2,600) to 1975 (26,000). The National Center for Education Statistics reports that women constituted 7.5 percent of the first-year class in 1969–70 and 23.4 percent of the first-year class in 1974–75. Several law schools have actively recruited women students. Those in urban centers, such as NYU in New York City, Rutgers in New Jersey, and Temple in Philadelphia, report that the percentage of women students in 1979 reached 50 percent, 50 percent, and 25 percent respectively. In addition, most law schools have women's groups that encourage women to enter the legal profession. The women at Rutgers publish a *Women's Rights Law Reporter Journal*, and women on other campuses have organized for mutual support, information, and as a lobby group for equal rights in the profession.[26]

From studies conducted in the 1970s, it appears that women students have been accepted on an equal basis with men. Women lawyers who went to law school in the 1970s did not feel that they were discriminated against, although they were apprehensive when they first entered school. In 1972 the Committee on Women in Legal Education of the American Association of Law Schools (AALS) conducted a study. Eighty-one of 124 AALS-accredited law schools responded to the questionnaire, which covered four areas: recruitment and admission, faculty, placement, and intra-school policy. The results of the study indicated that the status of women law students has improved in all areas. College undergraduate grade scores and LSAT scores for men and women applicants were about the same. Several law schools admitted that they gave special consideration to athletes and to Ivy League applicants; women made up an insignificant number in both cases. Forty percent of the schools reported active recruitment programs for women, supplemented by women's groups in many schools that carried on their own recruitment campaigns. For both men and women students the attrition rate was low. Reasons for leaving were similar: financial problems, inability to keep up with the academic work, change in career goals, and family problems.[27]

Despite this generally favorable situation, some problems still exist. Only about half of the law programs include a course on women in the law. In addition, there are few women law professors or members of the faculty to provide role models or a support system for women students. After completing the second year in a top law school, many of the best students are offered summer positions in prestigious law firms with the understanding that they will be hired after graduation. They can earn as much as $400 a week during the summer and $25,000 a year after graduation. Women are not well represented in these schools and seldom are offered these prestigious positions.[28]

As faculty members, women have made small gains. In accredited law schools in 1972, 18 deans or assistant deans were women, 243 were men. Women law faculty members composed small portions of the total: 18 percent of all faculty, mostly at the lowest level; 11 percent of the instructors (whereas men were 1 percent); and 2.54 percent of professors (Ruth Ginzburg of Columbia Law School became the first woman professor in 1972). Of the women faculty members, 21 percent were tenured, compared to 49 percent of the men. In the academic year 1978–79, out of a total of 5,535 full-time faculty in approved law schools, 820 (15 percent) were women. All the schools had similar teaching standards for men and women, and required research, writing, and some type of pro bono work.[29]

DISCRIMINATION

The degrees and types of discrimination increase as women move from school to active participation in the profession. Many firms are reluctant or unwilling to hire women. Students interviewing for their first jobs report that some firms, especially the largest and most prestigious ones, make it clear that they did not hire many women, did not make women partners, did not pay equal salaries for the same work, and did not give women the same work opportunities as men. A New York University Law School study done in 1970 found open discrimination. Women applying to private firms were told "We just hired a woman and couldn't hire another," or "We don't like to hire women," or were asked "Are you planning children?"[30] Around the same time women students at Columbia University sued the top 12 law firms in New York City to break their exclusionary policies against women; by 1976 several of the firms began to hire women.[31]

Being hired, however, is only the first step, and many women find that even after they enter a firm their path is not easy. Generally, they earn less than men for the same work. In 1970, Harvard University Law School, a leading source of lawyers for prestigious law firms, reported that 99 percent of the male students received two or more job offers but only 44 percent of the women did. A 1970 study of the graduates in the classes of 1953 to 1959 showed that 70 percent of the women working fulltime earned less than $20,000 a year, whereas only 16 percent of the men made less than that. James J. White conducted a study of 1,300 men and 1,300 women in 1967, all of the same graduating class. He reported that men earned $1,500 more than women in the first year, and after ten years men's median income was $8,300 higher than women's. Women were not often promoted and rarely were made partners. They also had little contact with clients and seldom participated in policy-making meetings or social gatherings with clients and colleagues. Women usually were assigned to do the legal research and the men went to court and tried the cases.[32]

White tried to determine the degree to which discrimination was based on objective factors. He found no scholastic difference between men and women in law schools; in fact, law schools reported that women usually worked harder than men, ranking among the top third of their class. He found no evidence that women are less motivated and dedicated than men, nor any proof that women either drop out or change careers after graduation any more than men. If they do, it is for the same financial and personal reasons as men. Most women also work full time after graduation.[33] (Bysiewicz in 1972 also reported that there were no differences in these areas.)

One way to avoid some of the discrimination is to open one's own law office, which in any case is the goal of many lawyers. In theory this option always has been open to women, but in fact it is open only to those few who have the money and contacts to start a business from the ground up. A law office requires books, insurance, secretarial help, and all the other expenses of any commercial operation. There must be a constant search for clients, a difficult task for women who are not part of the "old boys" network (as is evident when the male lawyers and judges meet informally in social situations from which women are excluded). There is still a strong belief among many clients that they will not get a fair trial if a woman represents them.[34]

Certain areas are considered appropriate for women, such as family law, estate law, legal aid and criminal law, legal research and documentation, and library work. These have relatively low status and income. White and Cynthia Epstein conducted studies on women in the legal profession and both confirmed this localization in "women's" specialties: trusts, estates, and domestic relations.[35]

Even those women who have gone into criminal law usually have not found their work very lucrative. Indeed, the low financial returns may be one reason why women faced little resistance from men when they began entering criminal practice at the turn of the century. As Clarence Darrow said, "You won't make a living at it, but it's worthwhile and you'll have no competition."[36] Clara Foltz was called the "Portia of the Pacific" because of her work as a criminal attorney in California. Marilla Ricker was the "Prisoner's Friend" because she defended poor prostitutes and criminals. Martha Strickland became assistant prosecuting attorney in Detroit. Laura DeForce Gordon achieved fame as a criminal attorney in California. Anna M. Kross, graduated from the New York University Law School in 1912, joined other women lawyers in defending prostitutes in the New York City Women's Night Court. Elizabeth Blume-Silverstein, who specialized in criminal law in Newark, New Jersey, at the turn of the century, was considered a "kook" because of her specialty. Perhaps they were jealous of the $100- to $200-a-day fee she received in 1913 when she started practice.[37]

In the quest for equal opportunity in jobs and money, women have been encouraged to enter government jobs because such employment is based on competitive examinations that objectively recognize ability. Government jobs also provide tenure, benefits, regular hours, and an opportunity to get promoted. In 1960 more women lawyers started to enter government than men.[38]

However, most of the women lawyers who enter government are hired at positions two grades lower than men and never catch up. For example, 30 percent of all federal workers are women, but in grades 12, 13, and 14, less than five percent are women. As top level administrators in grades 15 through 18, women comprise less than one percent. In 1977, the U. S. Justice Department had a total of 1,611 assistant attorneys, of whom 163 were women.[39] A few women have key positions in policy making in the Defense Department, although according to Jill Wine, former assistant special prosecutor at the Watergate trials, and the Army's general counsel, they are still asked, "What's a pretty girl like you doing in a place like this?"[40] On the other hand, Deanne Siemer, the Defense Department's general counsel, who graduated at the top of her Harvard Law School class in 1968 and had been a trial lawyer and partner in a Washington, D.C. law firm, said that she had no difficulty as the highest ranking woman in the Pentagon: "People know me, I have no problem at all being a woman here."[41]

THE JUDGES

Similar patterns of discrimination are evident in appointing judges. The first woman judge was Marilla Ricker, appointed U. S. commissioner by the judges of the District of Columbia trial court in 1884, only two years after she was admitted to the Washington, D.C. bar. Carrie Kilgore, who sued the University of Pennsylvania to force it to admit her and other women, became the first woman master in chancery in Philadelphia in 1886, three years after she graduated from the university. Catherine McCulloch was elected justice of the peace in Evanston, Illinois in 1907. However, women had to wait until after the passage of the nineteenth amendment to be eligible for elective judgeships in most states.[42]

In 1977 there were 9 women on the highest state appellate courts and 18 on intermediate appellate courts. All told, in the 50 states there were 130 women judges, 2.5 percent of the total of 5,155 judges, in general jurisdiction courts; and in courts of limited jurisdiction there were 317 women, 5.8 percent of the total of 5,452 judges. Up to 1970 the overall percentage of women judges matched the percentage of women lawyers: 1.5 percent in 1960 and 4 percent in 1970. By 1978 women were 9.3 percent of all lawyers, and 5.8 percent of all judges. In 1977, including justices of the peace, there were 916 women judges out of 15,824, or 5.8 percent; excluding justices of the peace, women were only 4 percent of judges.[43]

Women judges often are assigned to certain jurisdictions that are traditionally considered the specialty of women, such as municipal or domestic courts that have little status, are not arenas for important cases, and provide few contacts for persons seeking a political career. About 12.4 percent of the judges in family courts are women, twice the rate of women on any other limited jurisdiction court.[44]

Some women have resisted sexual stereotyping. Florence Allen, elected to the Common Pleas Court in Cleveland in 1920, was told by her fellow judges (all men) that she was to have a special division created for her: divorce judge. She informed them that the voters who elected her expected her to keep her campaign promises to improve the inefficient criminal court, and therefore she could not accept the judges' offer. In the end they learned to treat her as an equal, but only when court was in session.[45]

Another case is that of Marie M. Lambert, who broke the male monopoly over surrogate court judgeships in New York City. The surrogate court judge appoints lawyers to handle estates and act as guardian over estates of individuals held incompetent to oversee their own affairs. The executor of the estate receives a fee and the judges decide who will be the executor. The judges are carefully selected by political and legal elites to insure that the power goes to the proper persons. Until 1977, men controlled that court. In 1977 Lambert won election to the Manhattan Surrogate Court, despite the fact that the male-dominated New York Bar Association rated her "not approved."[46]

At the federal level, no woman has served on the U. S. Supreme Court. Until 1979, a total of only 12 women have ever served on other federal benches, 10 of them serving at various periods from 1920 to 1970; in 1977 there were 7 women serving on a federal bench. Two women have sat on the U. S. Court of Appeals: in 1934 Florence E. Allen was appointed chief judge of the Sixth Circuit, and in 1968 Shirley M. Hufstedler was appointed to the Ninth. In 1978 one of the 97 appeals judgeships was held by a women, and all told 6 of 525 federal judges were women.[47]

The limited number of women on the bench does not necessarily stem from a lack of qualified women. A Justice Department criterion that a person must have 15 years of experience as a practicing attorney to be considered for a judgeship excludes most women and minority group members who are relative newcomers to the law. Mildred Jeffrey, chairperson of the National Women's Political Caucus, said:

> The process of selecting federal judges is a disaster for women. At every stage of the selection process we have found well-qualified women excluded or overlooked. The President must take charge immediately to get more women on the bench.[48]

In 1978 Congress enacted the omnibus judgeship bill that increased the number of federal judges by 25 percent by creating 152 new judgeships. It was hoped that women and minority members would have an opportunity to gain entrance into the federal judicial system. However, the old obstacles remained. In addition, selection panels usually did not include women. Senator Jacob Javits's six member panel had no women, and President Jimmy Carter's panels had no women as chairs and no women's bar association was asked to contribute.[49]

Appointments were finally made. In March 1979 the Senate confirmed the judgeship of Phyllis Kravitch, a Georgia Superior Court judge in Savannah, to the Court of Appeals for the Fifth Circuit. In May 1979 Amalya L. Kearse was confirmed for the Second Circuit U. S. Court of Appeals. Kearse had been the first woman the first black to become a partner in one of the leading Wall Street law firms. Ann Thompson, prosecutor of Mercer County, New Jersey, a black and a former municipal judge, has been nominated for a federal judgeship.[50]

These general efforts, although important and effective in their own way, affect only a few women; most women lawyers with aspirations to judgeships will have to find other avenues. In considering this problem, one researcher has developed a theoretical model of the kinds of things women must do. Beverly Blair Cook, a political scientist at the University of Wisconsin, Milwaukee, argues that women must achieve what she calls the "manifest offices," positions that historically have been sources of candidates for judgeships: U. S. district attorney, state district attorney, private practice trial work, and membership of a legislature. Until recently women rarely have been allowed access to another route, clerkship under prominent judges; but in 1975, 14.4 percent of such clerkships were held by women.[51]

DIVISION OVER GOALS

Even as women have been fighting discrimination in the various levels and branches of legal education and practice, they have been trying to define their own roles as lawyers more clearly. This has become particularly urgent during the past 20 years, as federal laws have helped break down many of the traditional barriers against women in the profession. Women lawyers may be divided into two broad groups: the diplomats and the fighters. The diplomats, who prefer to work within the system and through channels, believe that discrimination is best dealt with by working harder to gain the respect of men. Separate women's professional organizations, they argue, segregate women and make them stand out. The fighters blame the diplomats for the low salary, low status, and limited opportunities women face in the profession. They accuse the diplomats of accepting whatever is given to them by men in the profession and even of joining with men in putting down women lawyers and judges.[52]

The diplomats appear to be losing ground. As more women enter law school and pass the bar, fewer are willing to take a back seat in their chosen profession. Law schools have women's groups that work against discrimination in the academic end of lawyering. Women's divisions of local and national bar associations work against discrimination. The National Women's Political Caucus, the National Organization of Women, and other women's groups have organized in some cities to lobby for the appointment of women judges. Women also have the support of the National Association of Women Lawyers (NAWL), the section of women in the Association of American Law Schools, the American Association for Higher Education, the Association of American Colleges, and the American Association of University Professors. They have been publishing the *Women Lawyers Journal* for almost a century, and the articles reflect the change in attitude of the women; they have become fighters.

Yet another divergence among women lawyers is over the degree to which women should remain in the traditional areas of family and juvenile law. The diplomats' view was ably set forth in 1960 by Neva B. Talley, then president of the National Association of Women Lawyers. She said that as more women entered employment outside the home they would seek out women lawyers, feeling "that a successful professional woman can better understand their feminine fears and hesitations."[53] Women's unique instincts made them especially suitable for certain areas of law, as well as for protecting society against the evils of subversion:

> Just as the female of the animal species in the jungle is first to hear faint noise of an approaching enemy and be instantly alerted to protect her young, also the woman is more likely the first to hear the faint whimper from the baby's cradle when he has kicked loose his cover on a cold winter night. Should we not use these innate tendencies of alertness to support and strengthen our form of government?[54]

A woman lawyer should "cater to the demand and capitalize on the fact that she is a woman trained in the field of law, but not a 'feminist' in the general conception of extreme female tendencies."[55] In effect, Talley told women lawyers to know and keep their place in society and in the law.

In 1969, the NAWL met in Dallas to celebrate the centennial of women in the legal profession. According to Marjorie Childs, national chairperson of the Women Lawyers Centennial and referee of the Juvenile Court of the City and County of San Francisco, "The climax of women lawyers' achievements during the centennial year" was the election of the NAWL's past president, Neva B. Talley, as chairman of the family law section of the American Bar Association (ABA). Childs believed that although Talley had worked for the section for many years, her election to the chair of an important ABA section was a major recognition of the work of women in the profession.[56] It is significant that Talley, a woman, was appointed to the family law section.

At the same meeting, questions arose on the place of women in the legal profession. Are they women lawyers and judges or are they lawyers and judges? Judge Sarah T. Hughes questioned the need for a separate women's bar association:

> Would it not be better to work with men? It would be harder to accomplish some of our goals, but wouldn't it be more worth while?

> When we did get somewhere, we would have gotten there together and
> not just be a group of women who did something.[57]

She was answered by Margerite Rawalt of the District of Columbia Bar,
who strongly disagreed: "We've gotten to the place where women have to
become militant to get anywhere."[58] She was supported by many, among
them Democratic Representative Martha Griffiths of Michigan, who
believed that women have to unite to fight inequities in the legal system.

The majority of the women at the NAWL centennial meeting
supported the concept and fact of a separate women lawyers association.
Speaking for the majority, NAWL president Jettie Pierce Silvig stated,
"When we finally attain true equality in the law and under the law, then
and only then will the need for our organization cease to exist."[59]

THE FUTURE

The dialogue among women about their proper role in law is a sign
that the future of women in the legal profession will not be a simple
matter of "onward and ever upward." Progress cannot be measured solely
in numbers, for this ignores the qualitative aspects of careers. This
mistake has been made, for example, in a recent article in the *Wall Street
Journal*, entitled "Ladies of the Bar: Women Attorneys, Now Over 9% of
Profession, Keep Making Gains in All Areas of Legal Work." The author,
noting that women have made "significant strides," speculates that "law
may become the first traditionally male profession to achieve full sexual
integration."[60] In sheer numbers this position has some support. In 1910
women lawyers were 1 percent of the total number in the profession; in
1948 they were 1.8 percent; in 1963 they were 2.8 percent; in 1970 they
were 2.8 percent; in 1975 they were 4 percent; and in 1978 they were 9.3
percent. In 1975 there were about 16,000 women lawyers of a total of
400,000 lawyers. In 1978 there were about 41,000 women lawyers of a
total of 441,000 practicing attorneys. But the figures are not nearly so
impressive when compared to the total proportion of women in the U.S.
population, over 50 percent, and in the total U.S. work force, over 40
percent. Taking into account the general rise of women in law schools (25
percent of law students in 1978), it is possible that by the year 2000
women will constitute about 25 percent of all lawyers, hardly "full sexual
integration."[61]

In any case, the "old boys" network will continue to exert its
incalculable influence, even when there is an "old girls" network
alongside it. Men will no doubt still get the first chance at the good jobs,
the best referrals of clients, and the legal positions most likely to lend
status and open the way for political ambitions. Politicians will continue

to offer rhetoric about equality during elections and then tread water once they enter office. Mayor Edward Koch of New York City promised to reduce discrimination in the courts. Although he did indeed appoint a woman to the Criminal Court in Queens, the lowest court in the criminal judicial system, he also appointed two other women to the Family Court, precisely the kind of work that has been stereotyped as women's domain.[62]

The real impetus for change therefore will come not from without but, continuing a century-long tradition, from women lawyers themselves as they arrive at a consensus of what their role should be. This self-reliance and need for defining one's goals, not having them defined by others, is summed up by Helene Schwartz in her autobiography:

> I was held back because I am a woman. Worse yet, I did not recognize that I was being held back.... The growth of the women's movement led to an awakening in me of what I might hope to accomplish as a lawyer, and for this the movement has my everlasting gratitude.[63]

NOTES

1. Kathleen E. Lazarou, "Fettered Portias: Obstacles Facing Nineteenth-Century Women Lawyers," *Women Lawyers Journal* 64 (Winter 1978): 21–22; Julia C. Spruill, *Women's Life and Work in the Southern Colonies* (New York: Norton Library, 1972), pp. 236–41; and Robert E. Reigel, *American Feminists* (Lawrence, Kan.: University Press of Kansas, Kansas paperback, 1968), p. 135.

2. D. Kelly Weisberg, "Barred From the Bar: Women and Legal Education in the United States, 1870–1890," *Journal of Legal Education* 28 (1977): 494–99; Frances E. Willard and Mary A. Livermore, eds., *American Women: Fifteen Hundred Biographies* (1893; reprint ed., Detroit: Gale Research, Book Tower, 1973), vol. 1, pp. 10, 87–88, 94, 115, 117, 211, 283–84, 286, 293–94, 326–27, 339 and 350–52; vol. II, pp. 460, 468–69, 484, 487, 531, 557, 571, 609, 699, 718, 737, 759, 768, and 789; *Notable American Women 1607–1950: A Biographical Dictionary* (Cambridge, Mass.: Belknap Press, 1971), vol. I, pp. 188–90, and 651–52; vol. II, pp. 36–37, 329–30, 356–57, 492–93, and 606–7; vol. III, pp. 121, 540–41, and 590–92; and *For the Better Protection of Their Rights: A History of the First Fifty Years of the Women's Legal Education Society and the Woman's Law Class at New York University* (Washington Square, N.Y.: New York University, 1940), pp. 3, 7, and 9–11.

3. Eleanor Flexner, *Century of Struggle: The Woman's Rights Movement in the United States* (New York: Atheneum, 1971), pp. 29, and 122–24.

4. Willard and Livermore, op.cit., and *Notable American Women*, op.cit. For page numbers, see note 2.

5. Lazarou, op.cit., p. 22; Reigel, op.cit., p. 135; and *Notable American Women*, op.cit., vol. II, pp. 492–93.

6. Lazarou, op.cit., pp. 23–24; Weisberg, op.cit., p. 489; and Karen DeCrow, *Sexist Justice* (New York: Vintage Books, 1975), pp. 30–31.

7. DeCrow, op.cit., pp. 30–33; and Leo Kanowitz, *Sex Roles in Law and Society: Cases and Materials* (Albuquerque, N.M.: University of New Mexico Press, 1973), pp. 43–44.

8. Lazarou, op.cit., p. 25; DeCrow, op.cit., pp. 34–35; and Weisberg, op.cit., p. 499.

9. Lazarou, op.cit., p. 25.

10. Ibid., pp. 25–26; Reigel, op.cit., p. 136; and Willard and Livermore, op.cit., vol. II, pp. 468–69.

11. Lazarou, op.cit., p. 21.

12. Ibid., p. 27; and Weisberg, op.cit., pp. 490–91.

13. Weisberg, op.cit., p. 499; and Reigel, op.cit., p. 136.

14. Weisberg, op.cit., p. 494; Lazarou, op.cit., pp. 28–29; Juvenal L. Angel, *Careers for Women in the Legal Profession* (New York: World Trade Academy Press, 1961), pp. 6–7, and 19; and Beatrice Doerschuk, *Women in the Law: An Analysis of Training, Practice and Salaried Positions* (New York: Bureau of Vocational Information, 1920), p. 36.

15. Lazarou, op.cit.; Angel, op.cit.; and Doerschuk, op.cit.

16. Lazarou, op.cit., p. 22; and Weisberg, op.cit., p. 494.

17. Weisberg, op.cit., pp. 486 and 494; Doerschuk, op.cit., pp. 19–27; also, see note number 2.

18. *For the Better Protection of Their Rights*, op.cit., pp. 3, 7, and 9–11.

19. Ibid., pp. 16–17.

20. Ibid., pp. 18–20.

21. Ibid., pp. 21–31.

22. *Notable American Women*, op.cit., vol. II, pp. 36–37, and 606–7.

23. Ibid.

24. Doerschuk, op.cit., pp. 19–20; Doris L. Sassower, "Women in the Law: The Second Hundred Years," *American Bar Association Journal* 57 (April 1971): 332; and Beatrice Dinerman, "Sex Discrimination in the Legal Profession," *American Bar Association Journal* 55 (October 1969): 951.

25. Doerschuk, op.cit., pp. 9–10, 22–25, 29, and 58.

26. "Project on the Status and Education of Women" (Washington, D.C.: Association of American Colleges, 1977), p. 4 (reprint); and Albie Sachs and Joan Hoff Wilson, "Sexism and the Legal Profession: A Study of Male Beliefs and Legal Bias in Britain and the United States," *Women's Rights Law Reporter Journal* 5 (Fall 1978): 64.

27. Shirley R. Bysiewicz, "1972 AALS Questionnaire on Women in Legal Education," *Journal of Legal Education* 25 (1973): 503–7.

28. Ibid., pp. 507–12.

29. Ibid., pp. 507–8; and information supplied by the American Association of Law Schools, August 1979.

30. Sassower, op.cit., p. 332.

31. Jim Drinkhall, "Ladies of the Bar," *Wall Street Journal*, May 31, 1978, p. 46.

32. Barbara S. Deckard, *The Women's Movement: Political, Socioeconomic, and Psychological Issues* (New York: Harper and Row, 1979), pp. 133 and 143; James J. White, "Women in the Law," *Michigan Law Review* 65 (April 1967): 1052–53, 1067, and 1093; and White, "Women in the Law," in *The Professional Woman*, ed. Athena Theodore (Cambridge, Mass.: Schenkman, 1971), pp. 647–59.

33. White, "Women in the Law," *Michigan Law Review*, and White, "Women in the Law," *The Professional Woman*.

34. Sachs and Wilson, op.cit., p. 67.

35. White, "Women in the Law," *Michigan Law Review*, p. 1062; and Cynthia F. Epstein, *Woman's Place: Options and Limits in Professional Careers* (Berkeley: University of California Press, 1970), pp. 153 and 160–62.

36. Quoted in Weisberg, op.cit., p. 497.

37. Willard and Livermore, op.cit., vol. I, pp. 294 and 327; vol. II, pp. 609 and 699; David Ward, "Women in the Law," *New Jersey Star Ledger*, February 26, 1979, p. 12; and

Clarice Feinman, "Imprisoned Women: A History of Women Incarcerated in New York City, 1932–1975," (Ph.D. diss., New York University, 1976), pp. 192–94.

38. Epstein, op.cit., p. 171.

39. Sylvia G. McCollum, "The Federal Government and Affirmative Action: A Default of Leadership," *Resolution* 1 (Summer 1975): 10–12; and Drinkhall, op.cit., p. 46.

40. Bernard Weinraub, "The Women Who Make Policy at the Pentagon," *New York Times*, December 4, 1977, p. 82.

41. Ibid.

42. Beverly B. Cook, "Women Judges: The End of Tokenism," in *Women in the Courts*, ed. Winifred L. Hepperle and Laura Crites (Williamsburg, Va.: National Center for State Courts, 1978), pp. 85–86.

43. Ibid., p. 88.

44. Ibid., p. 89.

45. Ibid.

46. Ibid., p. 103, footnote 11.

47. Ibid., pp. 87 and 102–3; and Susan Ness, "A Sexist Selection Process Keeps Qualified Women off the Bench," *Washington Post*, March 26, 1978 (reprint).

48. Martin Tolchin, "U. S. Search for Women and Blacks to Serve as Judges Is Going Slowly," *New York Times*, April 22, 1977, pp. 1 and 34.

49. Ness, op.cit.

50. *New York Times*, March 22, 1979, p. A7; and Tom Goldstein, "City Lawyer and Connecticut Judge Joining Circuit Court: Amalya Lyle Kearse," *New York Times*, June 25, 1979, p. B2.

51. Cook, op.cit., pp. 92–93.

52. Dinerman, op.cit., p. 954.

53. Neva B. Talley, "Women Lawyers of Yesterday, Today, and Tomorrow," *Women Lawyers Journal* 46 (Summer 1960): 22.

54. Ibid.

55. Ibid., p. 25.

56. Marjorie M. Childs, "The Women Lawyers Centennial," *American Bar Association Journal* 56 (January 1970): 70.

57. Quoted in Ibid.

58. Quoted in Ibid.

59. Quoted in Ibid.

60. Drinkhall, op.cit., p. 46.

61. Ibid.

62. *New York Times*, March 29, 1979, p. B1.

63. Helen E. Schwartz, *Lawyering* (New York: Farrar, Straus and Giroux, 1976), p. x.

— Six —

CONCLUSION

It is evident from the previous chapters that the history of women in the criminal justice system as criminals, correction officers, police officers, lawyers, and judges, has been governed largely by one massive, deep-seated, widely held stereotype: the madonna/whore duality. It has been taken for granted by most people over the course of Western history that women are basically different from men in certain socially defined ways, and that they therefore must be treated differently. For the most part it has been assumed that this difference implied inferiority, so that different treatment really meant protection and relegation to roles that men did not regard important enough to perform themselves. Women were ready sources of offspring, physical satisfaction, adornment, cheap labor, and entertainment. Paradoxically, these same inferior beings often were placed on a pedestal as incarnations of probity and virtue; this appeared in Europe as the cult of the Virgin Mary and in the United States as the cult of true womanhood. Women were both weak and vulnerable, yet pure and worthy of the highest regard.

This divided attitude, at the same time condescending, genuinely admiring, and callous, is reflected in the history of women who became professionals in the criminal justice system. They have been expected to adhere to "womanly" roles within the system in keeping with their "womanly" ability. As long as they remained in their prescribed roles, they were accepted in the system. Therefore, the earliest U.S. women to enter corrections and law enforcement would seem to have been departing from the straight path of womanly virtue, according to which nothing was to be done that brought them into contact with the dregs of society or with unseemliness of any kind. But in fact they avoided most criticism because they operated along clearly defined, traditional womanly roles; they were sisters and mothers, not guards and cops. Both the reformers and the first paid professionals used the madonna/whore duality to argue that women criminals required their own separate institutions, where a staff composed entirely of moral women would uplift the fallen to their proper place in society. Over the next century women carved out a small system of their own from which men were mostly excluded.

From the men's point of view, this was an agreeable arrangement. Segregation reduced the opportunities for women and eliminated direct competition between men and women for jobs, money and status, the things that men valued most highly. Women of great ability were given free rein within the women's system, but were not allowed into the men's, where the rewards were greater. Therefore women were automatically excluded from the top of the pyramid. Women quickly saw this disadvantage, but had no choice but to accept the arrangement at first.

In any case, the intellectual and psychological basis of the arrangement, the madonna/whore duality, was so widely held and so unquestioned by persons in authority that full integration with full equality was impossible. This was especially galling to women lawyers and judges, who were not so completely segregated as correction officers and policewomen and often could see very concretely how the duality limited their freedom to rise according to merit. Unlike women in corrections and law enforcement, women who entered the legal profession did not ask for separation nor proclaim their unique ability to protect and reform women and children. Rather, they assumed the right to practice law on an equal basis with men. Therefore, from the start, men viewed women lawyers as competitors and constantly placed obstacles in their paths to keep them from sharing the rewards of the profession: status, wealth, and power.

In the period after World War II, changes began that would produce the first serious challenge to the prevailing views. Middle-class women began entering colleges and professional jobs in unprecedented numbers; the civil rights movement of the 1960s raised fundamental questions of human freedom that could not be ignored; federal legislation and court decisions raised the possibility of social change through government action; and the women's movement provided the growing number of activist women with psychological support, theoretical arguments, and publicity. Out of all these simultaneous developments have come calls for the end of segregation and discrimination against women in the criminal justice system, on the argument that the old duality is not a true perception of women but a myth, a relic of the past that should not govern the present. The future, it is argued, should not be a continuation of the past and the present, but something new and different, based on equality of opportunity between men and women.

Such an argument has its pitfalls, of course, since it not only gives women equality, but also strips them of their old "privileges" and "protections." This is one of the prices of true independence and true adulthood, and it is unsettling to many people, even many women. Instead of the comfortable values of the often romanticized past, there is the uncertain promise of better things to come. And there is no guarantee that the day of full equality will ever come. Thus it is not surprising that women who favor integration and full equality have met enormous resistance, and will continue to do so.

Nevertheless, it is undeniable that changes have occurred, many of which have worked to women's benefit. However, the gains have been exaggerated. They exist mainly in legislation that guarantees women equal employment opportunity, not necessarily in the number of women entering the criminal justice system or advancing within the system. As of 1978, women constituted approximately 10 percent of the total number of correction officers, 3 percent of the total number of law enforcement officers, 9 percent of the total number of lawyers, 4 percent of the total number of judges (excluding justices of the peace), and about 1 percent of administrators in each of the fields. In addition, financial crises, tax revolts and budget cuts in cities and states, and court decisions upholding veterans' preference laws and inmates' rights to privacy have combined to limit the number of women in corrections and law enforcement and their equal employment opportunities. Furthermore, there has been an uneven distribution of these limited benefits among the components of the criminal justice system.

On the whole, those who work most closely with criminals have achieved the least progress, perhaps because of a literal guilt by association. There is no doubt that corrections is the least highly regarded component of the criminal justice system, not only by the public but also by legislatures. The budgets are low, training is poor, and working conditions, especially the "locked-in culture," are very demanding. This has been true from the very beginning in the mid-nineteenth century, and is likely to remain so because women in corrections are not well organized. There is no official organization or trade association to lobby on their behalf, either before legislatures or in the media.

The situation is much better for women in law enforcement, who generally are viewed as more professional than correction officers, perhaps because they retain much of their traditional social work identity. They also have much more occasion to meet the public, especially as members of rape, juvenile, and domestic violence task forces. In addition, they have their own national organization to speak on their behalf.

Lawyers have the best position of all women in criminal justice. They are the best educated, the most articulate and well organized, and often politically well connected. Their work is not physical, and they do not wear uniforms nor carry weapons, therefore, avoiding the taint of being called unwomanly or masculine. They also are able to share the generally high status associated with a nationally recognized profession. Within the profession, however, the position of women is more ambiguous. Until recently they were small in number and usually restricted, by custom, not law, to the least lucrative aspects of law practice. Only in the past decade have they made real, if limited, progress toward equality of opportunity.

At the other end of the system, the criminals, it is difficult to speak of any great improvement or hope of future equality with men. Somehow the terms seem inappropriate for persons who have been taken out of society and put behind bars. However, one can discuss the theories and ideas put forth by professionals in the criminal justice system to explain why women commit crime and what the future of that criminal pattern is. Here, too, the traditional views were tied to the madonna/whore concept, with its notion of a fall from grace and its emphasis on domesticity as the vehicle for rehabilitation. Little has changed in this regard. Equally important, the theories to explain the nature of female crime are no more rooted in fact now than 100 years ago, and with less excuse, because today at least there exist volumes of statistics and data. But chivalry is not dead, at least as a theory, and the masculinized woman offender lives on in the minds of many, both in and out of the criminal justice system.

Always, it seems, some researchers go out of their way to find exotic causes for criminal behavior of women, when many of the causes are apparent in poverty, ignorance, lack of opportunity, and the like. Perhaps this reluctance to recognize the facts is simply a way of avoiding the painful truth that women have been and continue to be discriminated against in the economic and professional arenas. It is far easier to blame the women's movement for everything, even new forms of criminal behavior that do not exist, then to look inward for the causes. The reluctance to face reality about women's criminality may serve another function: to reinforce the myth that the nonconforming woman is dangerous and criminal, the whore.

Similarly, many highly emotionally charged reasons have been given for denying women in corrections, law enforcement, and the law full integration and equal opportunity. The intensity of the madonna/whore duality argument is obvious in statements describing the women who want equality: unwomanly, sexually suspect, loose, physically weak, emotionally unstable, unreliable, and endangering the lives of correction and police officers and the legal cases of clients.

The intensity and emotionalism of the issues raised against women began in the 1960s when many women moved to achieve equal status in the criminal justice system and went to court for that right, and is thus directly related to their challenge to men's control of the system and its rewards. This relationship becomes clearer when one remembers that during World War II, when competition for jobs was not an issue, none of the above stated reasons was directed at keeping women out of non-traditional employment. Those arguments came after the war when men returned to civilian life and employment.

This will not be the first time that rationalization has been utilized to justify why one group has a near monopoly of wealth, power, and status. The emotionalism of the recent debate over the women's movement and the issues concerning the role of women in society and in the criminal justice system strongly suggests that traditionalists know how high the stakes are. If the past is any gauge to the future, those components of the criminal justice system that contain the most educated and articulate women will make the greatest strides toward equality of opportunity. The other components will lag behind, trailed only by the criminals.

However, despite their differences, women in the system continue to be bound by the persistence of traditional beliefs concerning their womanhood that deny them full acceptance and equality in society and the criminal justice system. Although limited gains in that direction have been made by professional women, full equality will not be a reality in the near future.

INDEX

California: Department of Corrections, 55; employment opportunity in, 55; Highway Patrol, 80; policewomen in, 76; prison in, 58
Calvert, Cecilius, 88
Calvert, Leonard, 88
Camp Retreat, 32
Carter, Jimmy, 100
Center for Women's Policy Studies, 50
Challenge of Crime in a Free Society, The, 26
check falsification, 19
Chessman, Lydia, 18
Chicago: detention center/prison in, 27; policewomen in, 71; prostitution in, 66; racial discrimination in, 53
Chicago Legal News, 90
children: abandoned, 69; care of, costs, 24; correctional facilities for, 43; illegitimate, 41; and incarcerated mothers, 50; and policewomen, 69, 71, 72; visiting privileges of, 32
Childs, Marjorie, 102
chivalry in criminal justice, 22–24
Christianity and infanticide, 3
Circuit Court of Appeals, Ninth U.S., 78
City of Philadelphia v. Pennsylvania Human Relations Commission, 57
Civil Rights Acts: 1957, 6; 1964, 54, 75, 95
Civil Service Commission, U.S., 73, 76
civil service requirements: and correction officers, 52–53; and policewomen, 73–74, 77–78
Cleveland: Common Pleas Court, 99; policewomen in, 76
Clinton, New Jersey, prison/reformatory in, 32–33, 45
Collins, Isaac, 43
Collins, Ruth, 47, 48
Colorado, prison in, 58
Columbia College, Washington, 90
Columbia University Law School, 93, 96; and sex discrimination, 97

Commissioner (Murphy), 74
Commission on Law Enforcement and the Administration of Justice, 26
Committee on Women in Legal Education of the American Association of Law Schools (AALS), 95
common law; sex roles in, 5; on women in law, 89–90, 91
Comprehensive Employment and Training Act (CETA), 31
computer banking and crime, 17
Connecticut: criminal sanctions in, 7; policewomen in, 71
Cook, Beverly Blair, 101
Corbin, Margaret, 18
Cornell University, 88
correction officers (matrons), 44–45, 49–52; morale of, 51; motives of, 51–52; salaries of, 51–52; status of, training of, 49–50 (see also corrections roles, women in)
corrections roles, women in, 39–64; correction officers (matrons), 44–45, 49–52; and discrimination (racial, 53; sexual, 53–58, and veterans, 52–53, 61); future of, 60–61; goals in, disagreement, 59–60; historical background on, 39–42; performance studies of, 58–59; reformers/activists, 39–46; superintendents, 46–48; theory and practice of, 42–46
Costello, Mary A., 7
Court of Appeals, U.S., 94, 100
Couzens, Phoebe W., 92
Craig, Glen, 80
credit cards and crime, 17, 19
Crime Control Acts, 1968, 54; 1973 and 1976, 75
crime statistics, extraneous factors in, 14–17
Crocker, Hannah, 88
"cult of true womanhood," 9, 40

Dallas, policewomen in, 76
Daniel, Jane, 7
Darrow, Clarence, 98

ABOUT THE AUTHOR

CLARICE FEINMAN is assistant professor of Criminal Justice at Trenton State College, New Jersey, and consultant for the New Jersey Department of Corrections Training Academy.

Dr. Feinman has published in the areas of criminal justice and history. Her articles and reviews have appeared in *Crime and Delinquency*, *Afro-Americans in New York Life and History*, and *Crime and Justice: A Historical Review*.

Dr. Feinman holds a B.A. from Brooklyn College and an M.A. and Ph.D. from New York University.